GRID ART

Volume 1: Animals

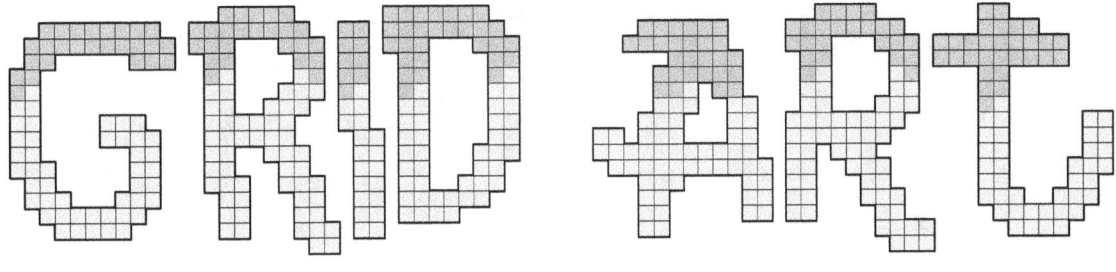

Volume 1: Animals

Robyn Broyles

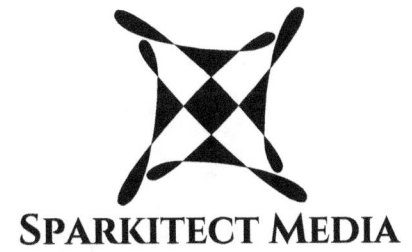

SPARKITECT MEDIA

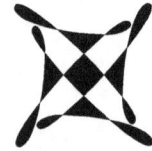

The Sparkitect Media name and logo are trademarks of Sparkitect Media.

GRID ART, VOLUME 1: ANIMALS

Cover design by Robyn Broyles.

Published by Sparkitect Media, Houston, Texas. Printing information for this book is found on the last page.

ISBN-13: 978-0692494417
ISBN-10: 0692494413

A.M.D.G.

To Rosy, my favorite "R" sister,
who shares my appreciation
for both art and mathematics.

And the whole is greater
than the part.

—Euclid

How to Have the Most Fun Coloring

This book contains 22 hidden scenes to color. Each one features a different kind of animal – masked by a geometric grid. Some of them are well-known creatures that everybody loves. Others are unusual beasts you may not have seen before. Some are familiar animals, but shown in a surprising way. And each figure is posed in realistic surroundings, such as the creature's natural habitat.

Some of the designs require more concentration than others. Each picture is marked with stars – the more stars, the harder it is to color!

Here are some tips to help you have the most fun coloring:

★ Color the lightest colors first. It will prevent the darker colors from smearing into the lighter colors, and it will make it easier to fix mistakes.

★ If you are using markers (especially permanent markers) or watercolors, place a sheet of paper under the picture you are coloring so that it does not leave marks on the picture under it.

★ If you are using paint, make sure you have a fine-tipped brush for coloring the small spaces on the grid. You might also want a medium-tipped brush for coloring larger areas.

Choosing Colors

These pictures were created to work well when colored with a set of 24 fine-tipped Bic Mark-it® Color Collection permanent markers. This product was chosen because it has delightful colors at a good value. Of course, you can use other markers if you like. You can also use colored pencils, crayons, or watercolors.

For each picture, there is a list of Suggested Colors. It includes an abbreviation for the Bic Mark-It® color that was used in the original design. If you are using something else to color the pictures, and you don't have all the colors on the Suggested Colors list, you can switch to the Back-Up Colors. The picture will still look great, even though it doesn't use the exact same colors as the original.

Bic Mark-It® Color Abbreviations

FG	Forest Green		TB	Tuxedo Black
KL	Key Lime		HA	Hot Aqua
MG	Margarita Green		MB	Misty Blue
YB	Yellow Blaze		BSB	Blue Skies Blue
SM	Summer Melon		OVB	Oceanview Blue
PePa	Peach Parfait		DSB	Deep Sea Blue
PF	Pink Flamingo		PlPu	Plumtastic Purple
PoPu	Polynesian Purple		DR	Desert Rose
PePi	Petal Pink		WB	Woodsy Brown
FP	Fandango Pink		HB	Honey Brown
RR	Rambunctious Red		THT	Tiki Hut Tan
SO	Sunset Orange		CNG	Cloud Nine Grey

What's the Picture?

You won't be able to tell what the picture is just from looking at the blank grid. But if you color it according to the directions, a striking animal scene will appear!

Every space (whether it's a square, triangle, hexagon, or diamond) in the grid contains a number. To reveal each design, fill in each space with the color that matches its number.

The grids are printed only on right-hand pages. This is so that no grid will be ruined by the colors from the other side bleeding through. It also makes it more convenient to remove pages from the book and display your work. Information about each picture is printed on the facing page to the left of it.

Many people want to be surprised by the picture, but others want to know what they are working on. So to keep the surprise from being spoiled, we tell you the subject of each picture in code.

In this code, 1 stands for A, 2 stands for B, and so on. On the right side of this page is a handy key to make it easier to decode the titles.

We hope these pictures inspire you to create your own grid art! In fact, at the end of the book, you will find blank grids to color any way you wish.

1	A
2	B
3	C
4	D
5	E
6	F
7	G
8	H
9	I
10	J
11	K
12	L
13	M
14	N
15	O
16	P
17	Q
18	R
19	S
20	T
21	U
22	V
23	W
24	X
25	Y
26	Z

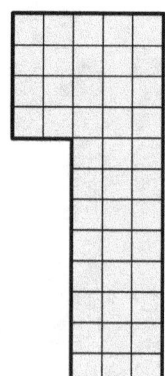

Suggested Colors

1	light green	MG
2	black	TB
3	yellow	YB
4	dark green	FG
5	light brown	THT

Back-up Colors

1	green
2	black
3	yellow
4	brown
5	orange

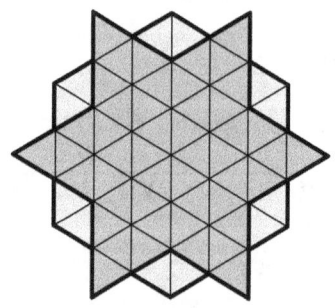

```
1 1 1 5 4 4 4 4 4 4 4 4 4 1 4 1 4 1 4 4 4 4 4 4 1 4 1 1
1 1 1 1 1 5 4 1 4 1 4 4 4 1 1 1 1 4 4 4 4 4 2 2 2 4 4
5 1 1 1 5 5 5 1 1 1 4 4 1 1 1 1 4 4 4 1 4 1 2 5 3 3 2 4
3 5 1 1 1 1 5 5 5 1 1 1 1 1 4 4 4 1 4 1 1 2 5 3 3 3 3 2
3 3 2 1 1 4 4 5 5 5 5 5 1 1 1 4 4 1 1 1 2 5 3 3 5 3 3 3
3 2 2 2 1 1 4 4 1 5 1 5 5 1 1 1 1 1 1 2 5 3 3 5 3 3 3 3
3 2 2 2 2 1 1 4 4 1 1 1 1 1 1 1 1 1 2 5 3 3 5 3 3 5 3 3
3 3 2 2 2 5 5 3 3 3 3 2 3 3 3 2 2 5 3 3 5 5 5 5 5 3 3 3
5 3 3 2 2 2 2 3 2 2 3 3 3 3 2 3 3 3 3 5 3 3 3 3 3 3 5 3
5 5 3 2 2 3 3 3 3 3 3 2 3 3 3 3 2 3 3 5 5 3 5 5 5 5 5 3
4 5 5 3 3 3 3 2 2 3 3 3 3 2 3 3 3 3 3 3 5 5 3 3 3 3 3 3
4 4 5 3 3 2 3 3 3 3 2 3 3 3 3 3 3 2 2 2 3 3 3 3 5 5 3 3
4 4 3 3 3 3 3 3 2 3 3 3 3 3 2 3 3 3 3 2 2 3 3 3 3 3 3 5
4 3 3 3 2 3 2 2 3 3 3 3 2 2 3 2 2 3 3 3 3 3 3 2 2 3 5 2
1 2 2 3 2 3 3 2 2 3 3 3 3 2 2 3 2 2 3 2 2 3 3 3 2 3 2 1
4 2 3 3 3 3 3 3 3 3 5 5 3 3 3 3 3 3 3 3 3 3 2 3 3 3 3 4
1 3 2 2 2 2 3 3 5 5 5 5 3 3 2 2 2 2 2 3 3 3 3 2 2 3 4
4 3 3 2 1 2 1 2 3 5 5 3 3 2 1 2 1 2 3 3 2 3 3 3 2 3 4
3 3 3 3 2 1 1 2 3 5 5 5 3 2 1 1 2 3 3 3 2 3 3 2 3 3 4
3 3 2 3 3 2 2 2 3 5 5 5 5 3 2 2 2 3 3 2 2 3 2 2 3 2 1
3 3 3 3 3 3 2 2 3 5 5 5 5 5 3 2 3 3 3 3 2 2 3 3 2 3 2 1
3 2 2 3 2 3 3 5 5 5 5 5 3 3 2 3 2 3 2 3 3 3 3 3 2 2 3 1
3 2 3 3 3 3 5 5 3 5 3 5 5 3 2 3 2 3 2 3 2 2 3 3 3 1
3 3 3 2 2 3 3 5 3 5 3 5 5 3 2 3 3 3 3 3 3 2 2 3 2 2
4 3 3 3 3 3 3 3 3 3 3 3 3 2 3 2 2 3 3 3 3 2 2 3 2 2
4 3 2 3 3 3 2 5 5 5 5 5 2 3 3 3 3 2 3 3 3 3 3 3 2 3
4 3 3 5 5 3 3 2 2 5 2 2 3 3 3 5 5 3 3 2 3 3 3 5 3 2
4 3 5 3 3 3 2 3 2 5 2 3 3 2 3 3 5 3 2 2 3 3 5 5 3 2
4 5 3 3 2 3 3 3 3 2 3 3 3 3 3 2 3 3 5 3 3 2 3 5 3 3 3
4 5 3 3 3 3 3 2 3 2 3 2 3 2 3 3 3 3 5 3 3 2 3 5 3 2 2
4 5 3 2 3 2 3 3 2 2 2 3 3 2 3 2 3 5 5 5 5 5 3 2 3 2
4 4 5 3 3 3 3 2 5 3 5 2 3 3 3 3 3 5 3 3 3 2 3 2 2 3
1 4 4 5 3 2 2 3 3 3 3 2 2 3 3 5 5 3 3 2 3 3 2 3 3 3
1 4 1 4 5 3 3 3 3 3 3 3 3 5 5 3 3 2 3 3 3 3 3 2 2 3
1 1 1 4 1 5 3 3 3 3 3 3 5 5 3 3 2 2 3 3 2 2 3 2 3 2 3
4 1 1 1 1 3 5 5 5 5 5 5 5 3 3 3 2 3 2 2 2 2 2 2 3
4 4 4 5 5 3 3 3 2 2 3 3 3 2 2 3 3 3 2 3 2 3 3 3 3 3
4 5 5 5 5 3 2 2 2 2 2 2 2 2 2 3 3 2 3 3 3 3 3 3 2 2
5 5 5 5 4 4 3 2 2 2 3 2 2 2 3 3 2 2 3 3 2 2 3 2 2 2
5 5 5 1 1 4 3 3 3 3 3 3 3 3 3 3 2 3 3 2 2 2 3 2 3 2 3
```

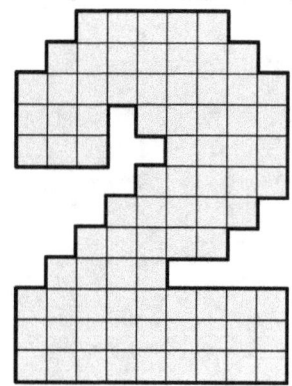

23-15-12-22-5-19

Suggested Colors

1	black	TB
2	red-orange	SO
3	light gray	CNG
4	dark brown	WB
5	light peach	PePa
6	dark green	FG

Back-up Colors

1	black
2	red
3	gray (or leave white)
4	brown
5	pink or orange
6	green

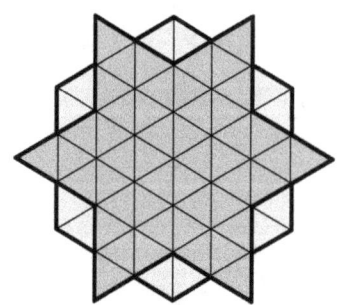

```
2 2 2 2 2 2 2 2 2 2 2 2 2 2 2 2 2 2 2 2 2 2 2 2 2 2 2 2 2 2 2 2 2 2 2 2
2 2 2 2 2 2 2 2 2 2 2 2 2 2 2 2 2 2 2 2 2 2 2 2 2 2 2 2 2 2 2 2 2 2 2 2
2 2 2 2 2 2 2 2 2 2 2 2 2 2 5 5 5 5 5 2 2 2 2 2 2 2 2 2 2 2 2 2 2 2 2 2
2 2 2 2 2 2 2 2 2 5 5 5 5 5 5 5 6 5 5 5 5 5 5 6 2 2 2 2 2 2 2 2 2 2 2 2
2 2 2 5 5 5 5 5 5 5 5 5 5 5 5 5 5 5 5 6 6 6 5 5 5 5 6 6 5 5 5 5 5 5 5 5
5 5 5 5 6 5 5 5 5 5 5 2 2 2 2 2 2 6 2 2 2 5 5 5 6 6 5 5 5 5 5 5 5 5 5 5
5 5 5 6 6 5 2 2 2 2 2 2 2 2 2 6 6 6 2 2 2 2 6 6 2 2 2 2 2 2 2 2 2 2 2 2
5 5 5 5 6 6 5 5 5 5 5 5 2 2 2 6 6 6 6 6 5 5 5 6 6 6 6 2 2 2 2 2 2 2 2 2
5 5 5 6 6 5 5 5 5 5 5 6 5 5 5 5 6 6 6 6 5 5 5 6 6 6 6 6 6 5 5 5 5 5 5 5
5 5 6 6 6 6 6 6 5 5 5 5 6 5 5 5 6 6 6 6 6 6 6 6 6 6 6 6 6 6 6 5 5 5 5 5
5 5 5 6 6 6 5 5 5 5 6 6 5 5 5 5 5 6 6 6 6 6 6 6 6 6 1 1 6 6 5 5 5 5 5 5
5 5 6 6 6 6 6 5 5 5 6 6 6 5 5 5 5 5 6 6 6 6 6 6 3 3 3 1 6 6 5 5 5 5 5 5
5 6 6 6 6 6 6 5 5 6 6 6 6 6 6 6 6 6 4 3 3 3 3 3 3 3 1 6 6 6 6 5 5 5 5 5
5 5 6 6 6 6 6 5 5 6 6 6 6 6 6 4 3 1 1 3 3 3 1 1 1 6 6 6 6 6 5 5 5 5 5 5
5 6 6 6 6 6 6 6 6 6 6 6 6 6 4 4 3 1 3 3 3 3 1 1 3 6 6 6 6 6 6 6 6 6 6 6
6 6 6 1 1 6 6 6 6 6 6 6 1 1 4 4 3 3 4 3 3 3 3 3 3 3 6 6 6 6 6 6 6 6 6 6
6 6 6 1 1 3 6 6 6 6 6 1 3 3 4 4 4 4 4 3 3 3 3 6 6 6 6 6 6 6 6 6 6 6 6 6
6 6 3 1 3 3 3 6 6 6 6 1 3 1 1 3 3 1 4 4 4 4 3 3 6 6 6 6 6 6 6 6 6 6 6 6
6 6 3 1 3 3 3 3 6 6 6 1 1 3 1 1 4 4 4 4 3 3 6 6 6 6 6 6 6 6 6 6 6 6 6 6
6 6 1 1 1 3 3 3 3 1 6 6 6 1 1 1 4 4 4 3 4 3 3 6 6 6 6 6 6 6 6 6 6 6 6 6
6 6 1 1 1 1 3 3 3 3 1 6 6 6 4 4 4 4 1 4 4 3 3 6 6 6 6 6 6 6 6 6 6 6 6 6
6 6 3 3 1 1 3 3 1 1 3 1 6 6 4 1 4 4 4 1 4 4 3 6 6 6 6 6 6 6 6 6 6 6 6 6
6 6 3 3 3 3 3 3 3 1 3 1 6 4 4 4 1 4 4 4 4 3 3 6 6 6 6 6 6 6 6 6 6 6 6 6
6 6 3 3 3 3 3 3 3 3 3 1 1 4 4 4 4 4 4 4 3 3 6 6 6 6 6 6 6 6 6 6 6 6 6 6
6 6 3 3 3 3 3 1 3 3 1 3 3 1 4 4 4 3 4 4 3 6 6 6 6 6 6 6 6 6 6 6 6 6 6 6
6 6 3 3 3 3 3 1 1 3 3 3 1 1 3 1 4 4 4 3 3 3 6 6 6 6 6 6 6 6 6 6 6 6 6 6
6 6 3 3 3 3 3 1 1 1 3 1 1 1 1 3 1 4 3 4 3 3 6 6 6 6 6 6 6 6 6 6 6 6 6 6
4 4 3 3 3 3 3 1 1 1 1 3 3 3 3 3 1 3 3 3 3 3 6 6 6 6 6 6 6 6 6 6 6 6 6 6
4 4 1 3 3 3 1 1 1 1 1 1 1 1 1 1 1 3 3 3 3 3 6 6 6 6 6 6 6 6 6 6 6 6 6 6
4 4 1 3 3 3 1 1 1 1 1 1 4 1 1 1 1 1 1 1 1 1 1 1 1 1 1 1 6 6 6 6 6 6 6 6
4 4 1 1 3 3 1 1 1 1 1 1 4 1 1 1 1 1 1 1 1 1 1 1 1 1 1 1 1 1 1 1 1 1 1 1
4 4 1 1 3 1 1 1 1 1 1 4 1 1 1 1 1 1 1 1 1 1 1 3 1 1 1 1 3 1
4 4 1 1 1 1 1 4 1 1 4 1 1 1 1 1 1 1 4 1 1 1 3 1 1 1 3
3 4 4 1 1 1 1 1 1 4 1 1 4 1 1 1 1 1 4 1 1 1 1 1 1 3
3 4 4 1 1 1 1 1 1 4 1 1 3 1 1 1 1 3 1 1 1 1 4 1 1
3 3 4 4 1 1 1 1 1 1 3 1 1 1 4 1 1 3 1 1 4 1 1 4 1 1
4 3 4 4 3 1 1 1 1 3 3 1 1 1 1 4 1 1 3 1 1 3 3 1 3 4 1
4 3 3 4 1 1 1 1 1 3 3 1 1 1 1 1 4 1 3 3 1 3 3 3 3 4 1
4 4 3 4 1 3 3 3 3 3 1 1 1 1 1 4 1 3 3 1 3 3 3 3 3 4 1
4 4 4 4 1 1 3 3 3 1 1 4 1 1 1 1 3 3 3 1 3 3 3 3 3 1 4
```

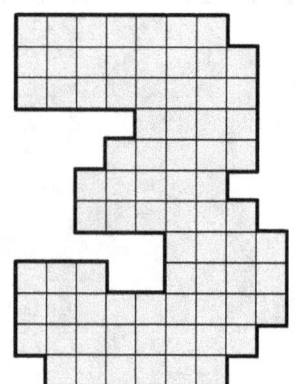

2-5-5-20-12-5

Suggested Colors

1	dark magenta pink	FP
2	dark green	KL
3	black	TB
4	yellow	YB
5	llight pink	PF
6	light blue	BSB

Back-up Colors

1	red
2	green
3	black
4	yellow
5	orange
6	blue

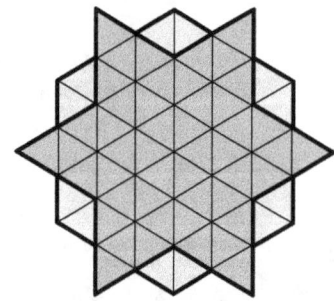

```
6 6 6 6 6 6 6 6 1 5 5 5 5 5 5 5 1 1 1 5 5 5 5 5 5 5 5 5 5 5
6 6 6 6 6 6 6 6 1 1 5 5 5 5 5 5 5 5 5 1 5 5 1 1 5 1 1 5 5
6 6 6 6 6 6 6 1 5 1 1 1 5 5 5 5 5 5 5 1 1 5 5 1 1 1 1 5 5 5
6 6 6 6 6 6 1 5 5 5 5 5 5 5 1 5 5 5 5 5 1 1 1 5 5 1 1 1 5 5 5
6 6 6 6 6 1 5 5 5 5 5 5 5 1 1 5 5 5 5 1 1 1 5 5 1 1 1 1 1 5 5
6 6 6 6 6 1 5 5 5 5 5 5 1 1 1 1 5 1 1 1 5 5 5 5 1 5 5 5 5 1
6 6 6 6 6 1 1 1 1 1 5 5 5 1 1 5 1 5 1 1 5 5 5 5 5 5 5 5 1 1
6 6 1 1 1 1 1 5 5 5 5 5 5 5 5 5 5 1 5 1 1 1 1 1 5 5 1 5 1 5
1 1 5 5 5 1 1 5 5 5 5 5 5 5 3 3 3 3 1 5 5 5 1 1 1 1 1 1
5 1 1 5 5 5 1 5 5 5 5 5 1 3 3 3 2 3 3 3 5 5 5 5 5 5 5 1
5 5 5 5 5 5 5 1 1 5 5 1 3 3 3 2 3 3 3 3 3 3 5 5 5 5 5 5
5 5 5 5 5 1 5 5 5 1 1 3 3 2 3 3 3 3 3 3 3 3 3 1 1 5 5 5
5 5 5 5 5 1 1 1 5 5 3 3 2 3 3 3 3 3 3 2 3 3 3 3 1 5 5 5 1
1 5 5 5 5 5 1 1 1 3 3 2 2 3 2 3 2 3 2 3 3 3 3 3 3 5 5 1 1
1 1 1 5 5 1 1 1 3 3 2 2 3 2 3 2 2 2 3 3 3 3 3 3 5 1 1 1 5
6 1 5 5 5 5 5 3 2 2 2 2 2 2 3 1 2 3 3 3 3 2 3 5 1 5 5
6 1 5 5 5 5 1 3 3 2 2 2 2 2 3 2 2 3 3 3 3 3 3 5 5 1 1 5 5
6 1 1 5 5 1 1 3 2 2 2 2 3 2 2 3 3 3 2 3 3 2 3 5 1 1 1 5
6 6 1 1 1 3 3 2 2 2 3 3 2 2 3 2 2 3 3 3 3 1 1 1 5 5 5
6 6 1 5 5 5 3 2 2 2 3 2 3 2 2 2 2 3 3 3 2 3 1 1 1 5 5 5
6 1 1 1 5 3 2 2 4 3 2 2 3 3 3 2 2 3 3 2 3 1 5 5 1 1 5 5
1 1 5 5 1 3 2 4 3 3 3 3 2 4 3 3 3 3 3 1 5 5 5 5 1 5 5
5 5 5 3 3 3 4 3 2 2 2 3 2 4 3 3 3 2 3 1 5 5 5 5 1 1 1
5 5 3 3 1 3 3 2 2 4 4 2 4 3 2 4 3 3 3 5 1 5 5 5 1 1 5 5
5 3 1 1 1 3 3 2 4 4 4 4 2 4 3 3 3 3 5 1 1 5 1 5 5 5 5 5
5 5 5 1 1 1 3 2 2 4 4 4 4 2 3 3 3 3 3 3 5 5 1 1 5 5 5 5 5
1 5 5 1 5 1 3 2 2 2 4 4 2 3 3 5 5 3 3 3 3 1 1 1 1 5 5 5
1 1 5 1 3 3 3 3 2 2 2 2 3 3 5 5 5 1 5 5 3 3 1 1 5 5 1 5
5 1 1 3 5 5 1 3 3 3 2 3 3 3 3 5 5 1 5 5 5 5 5 3 5 5 5 1 1
5 5 5 5 5 5 3 3 2 2 3 3 1 1 3 3 1 1 1 5 5 5 5 5 5 5 5 1
5 5 5 5 5 1 3 3 2 3 3 1 5 1 1 3 5 5 1 5 5 5 5 5 5 5 5 5
5 5 5 5 5 3 5 3 3 3 3 5 5 5 1 3 5 5 1 5 5 5 5 1 5 5 5 5 5
5 5 5 3 1 5 5 5 5 5 3 5 3 5 3 5 5 5 5 1 5 5 1 5 5 5 5 5
5 1 5 5 5 1 5 5 5 5 5 3 5 5 1 5 5 5 5 1 1 1 5 5 5 5 5
1 1 5 5 1 1 1 5 5 1 3 1 1 1 1 1 5 1 1 1 1 5 5 1 1 1 1 1
6 6 1 1 1 5 5 1 1 1 5 5 5 1 1 1 5 1 1 1 1 5 5 5 5 1 1
6 6 6 1 5 5 5 5 5 5 5 5 5 1 5 5 5 5 1 5 1 1 1 5 5 5 5 1
6 6 1 5 5 5 1 1 1 5 5 5 5 1 5 5 5 5 5 5 5 1 5 5 5 5 5 1
6 6 1 5 5 5 1 1 1 5 5 1 5 1 1 5 5 5 5 5 5 5 5 5 5 5 1 1
6 6 6 1 5 5 5 5 5 5 5 1 1 1 5 5 5 5 1 1 5 5 5 5 5 1 1 1
```

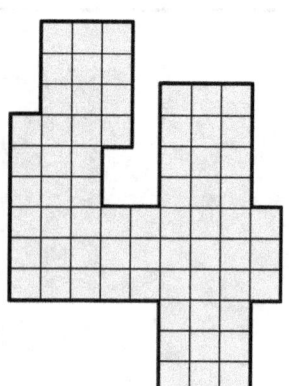

Suggested Colors

1	dark purple	DR
2	black	TB
3	green	FG
4	gray	CNG
5	yellow-orange	SM
6	red-orange	SO

Back-up Colors

1	purple
2	black
3	green
4	brown
5	yellow
6	orange

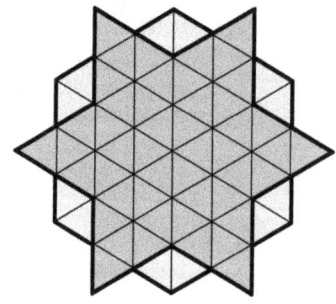

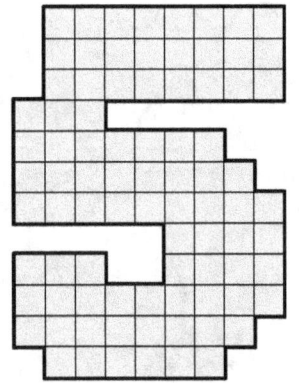

6-12-1-13-9-14-7-15-19

Suggested Colors

1	black	TB
2	pink	PF
3	blue-green	HA
4	brown	HB
5	red	RR
6	dark blue	DSB
7	green	KL
8	gray	CNG

Back-up Colors

1	black
2	orange
3	green
4	brown
5	red ··
6	blue
7	yellow
8	gray or brown

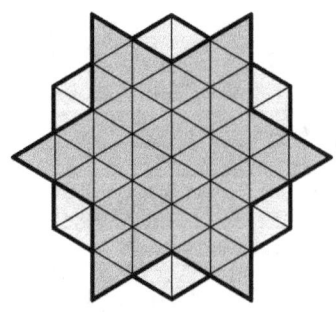

```
7 7 7 7 4 7 4 7 7 7 4 4 7 7 7 4 7 7 4 4 4 4 4 7 7 7 4 4
4 7 7 7 4 7 4 7 7 7 4 7 7 7 7 4 7 7 4 4 4 4 4 7 7 7 4 4
4 4 7 4 4 7 4 7 7 7 2 2 2 7 7 4 4 7 4 4 4 4 4 7 7 4 4 4
7 4 4 4 7 7 4 7 7 2 2 2 2 2 7 7 4 4 4 4 4 1 4 4 7 4 4 7
7 7 7 4 7 7 4 4 7 2 2 7 2 1 2 7 4 7 7 4 1 1 1 4 4 4 4 7
8 8 8 4 8 7 7 4 7 2 2 7 7 2 8 7 4 7 7 4 1 1 1 4 4 4 4 7
1 1 1 4 8 8 2 2 5 2 2 2 7 8 1 7 4 7 7 4 4 1 1 4 4 4 7 7
6 6 1 1 1 2 2 2 2 5 2 2 2 1 1 7 4 7 7 4 4 4 4 4 4 4 7 7
6 6 6 6 2 2 2 2 2 2 5 2 2 2 7 7 4 7 7 7 4 4 4 4 4 7 7 7
3 3 6 5 5 5 5 2 2 2 2 2 2 2 2 8 4 8 8 8 4 4 4 4 4 7 7 7
3 3 2 2 2 5 5 5 5 5 5 2 2 2 1 1 1 1 8 4 4 4 4 4 4 7 7
3 2 2 2 2 2 2 2 2 2 2 2 3 6 6 6 1 1 4 4 4 4 4 4 8 8
2 2 5 5 3 2 2 2 2 2 2 2 2 6 6 3 3 6 6 6 6 4 4 4 4 1 1
2 5 5 3 3 3 3 1 1 1 3 6 6 6 6 6 6 6 3 3 6 4 4 4 4 6 6
3 3 3 3 3 3 3 1 1 6 6 6 3 3 6 6 3 3 6 6 6 4 4 4 4 6 6
6 6 3 3 3 3 1 1 1 3 3 3 3 2 2 2 2 2 2 2 6 6 6 6 6 3 3
3 3 3 3 3 3 1 3 1 6 6 3 3 2 2 2 2 2 2 2 2 2 6 3 3 3 6 6
3 6 6 3 3 3 1 3 1 1 3 2 2 2 2 2 2 2 2 2 2 2 6 6 3 3 3
6 6 3 3 3 1 1 3 3 1 3 2 2 2 2 2 2 2 5 5 2 2 6 6 6 6
3 3 3 3 3 1 3 3 3 1 1 2 2 2 2 2 2 5 5 5 2 2 2 2 3 3 3
3 6 6 6 3 1 3 3 3 3 1 2 2 2 2 5 5 5 5 2 2 2 2 2 2 6 3
6 3 3 3 3 1 3 3 3 1 3 2 2 2 2 2 2 2 2 5 5 2 2 2 6
3 3 3 3 3 1 3 3 3 3 3 2 2 2 2 2 2 2 3 3 5 5 2 2 3
6 6 3 3 3 3 3 3 3 3 3 3 3 2 2 2 3 1 1 1 3 6 6 6 5 5 3 6
3 3 6 6 3 3 3 3 3 3 3 3 2 2 2 3 1 3 1 1 3 6 6 6 6 6
6 6 3 3 3 3 3 3 2 2 2 3 2 2 2 3 3 1 3 3 1 1 3 3 3 3 6 6
3 6 6 6 3 3 3 2 2 2 2 2 2 2 3 3 1 3 3 3 1 1 6 6 3 3 3
6 6 6 3 6 6 3 2 2 2 3 2 2 2 3 3 1 3 3 3 1 3 3 3 6 6
6 6 6 6 3 3 2 2 2 3 3 3 3 3 3 3 1 3 3 6 6 1 6 3 3 3 6
3 3 6 6 6 6 2 2 2 3 3 6 6 3 3 3 3 1 3 3 3 1 3 6 3 6 6 6
6 6 6 3 3 3 2 2 2 3 3 3 3 3 3 1 3 3 3 3 1 3 3 3 3
3 3 3 3 6 6 3 2 1 2 6 3 6 6 3 3 3 3 1 3 3 3 3 1 3 3 3 6 6
6 6 6 6 3 3 3 2 2 2 3 6 6 3 3 3 3 1 3 3 3 3 1 3 3 3 3 3
3 3 3 3 3 3 3 8 8 3 3 6 6 3 3 3 3 1 3 3 3 3 3 3 3 3 3 3
6 6 6 6 3 6 6 8 1 3 3 3 3 3 3 3 3 3 3 1 3 3 3 3 3 3 3 3
6 6 6 6 6 3 3 1 1 1 3 6 6 6 3 3 3 1 3 1 1 3 3 3 2 3 3
3 3 6 6 6 6 6 3 3 3 3 3 3 3 3 3 3 2 2 2 2 3 3 3 2 2 3 3
6 3 3 6 3 3 3 8 8 3 6 6 3 3 3 2 2 2 2 2 2 2 2 2 2 3 3 3
6 6 6 6 6 6 8 8 3 3 3 3 3 3 2 2 2 2 2 2 2 2 2 2 2 3 3 3
3 3 3 3 3 3 3 2 2 3 3 3 3 3 2 2 2 2 2 2 2 2 2 2 2 3 3 3
```

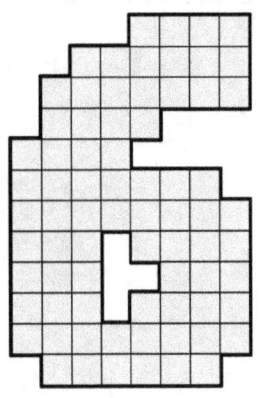

22-1-13-16-9-18-5

2-1-20-19

Suggested Colors

1	gray	CNG
2	brown	WB
3	light purple	PoPu
4	peach	PePa
5	black	TB

Back-up Colors

1 brown
2 orange
3 purple
4 pink or red
5 black

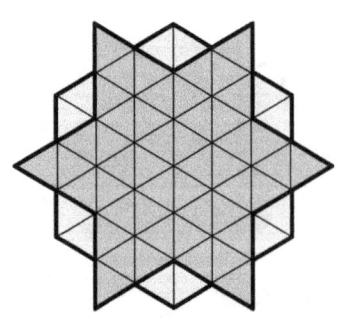

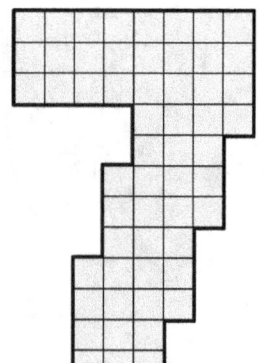

8-15-18-19-5

Suggested Colors

1	gray	CNG
2	light blue	OVB
3	black	TB
4	yellow	YB
5	brown	WB
6	green	KL

Back-up Colors

1 gray (or leave white)
2 blue
3 black
4 yellow
5 brown
6 green

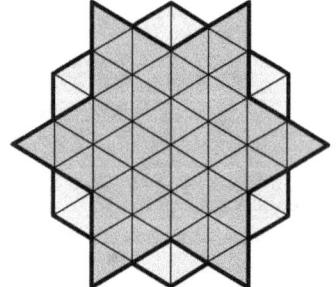

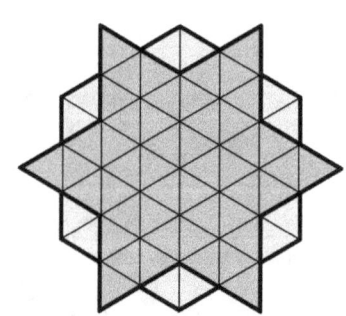

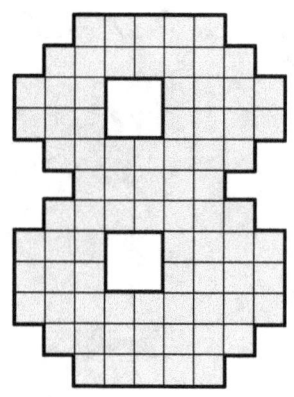

16-15-9-19-15-14

4-1-18-20   6-18-15-7

Suggested Colors

1	dark green	FG
2	purple	PlPu
3	red	RR
4	yellow	YB
5	light blue	OVB
6	orange	SO
7	midnight blue	DSB
8	light green	MG

Back-up Colors

1	green
2	purple
3	red
4	yellow
5	blue
6	orange
7	black
8	brown

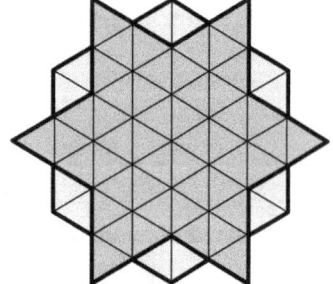
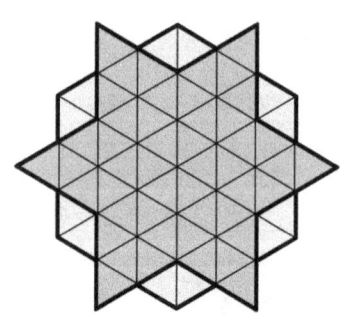

```
5 1 1 5 5 5 5 3 4 5 5 5 5 5 5 5 5 1 1 5 2 4 4 4 2 4 4 2
5 1 1 4 5 5 5 3 3 4 5 5 5 5 5 5 5 1 1 2 2 2 4 4 4 4 4 2
5 1 1 3 4 4 5 3 3 4 5 5 5 5 4 4 1 1 2 4 4 4 4 8 4 4 2 2
1 1 1 5 3 4 4 5 3 3 4 4 4 4 3 5 1 1 5 2 4 4 4 4 4 4 4 2
1 1 5 5 3 3 4 4 3 4 4 3 3 3 5 5 1 1 5 5 2 2 4 4 2 4 4 4
1 1 5 5 5 3 3 4 4 3 3 3 3 5 5 5 1 1 5 5 1 2 4 4 2 2 2 2
1 1 4 5 5 3 3 3 4 3 3 3 5 5 5 1 1 2 2 5 1 2 4 2 5 5 1 1
1 5 3 4 5 5 3 3 3 3 3 5 5 4 4 1 2 4 4 2 1 2 2 2 2 5 1 1
1 5 5 3 4 5 3 3 3 4 4 4 4 3 5 1 2 4 4 2 2 2 4 4 2 1 1 1
1 5 5 3 4 4 5 3 4 3 3 3 3 5 5 1 2 2 4 4 2 4 4 4 2 1 1 5
1 5 5 3 3 4 4 4 3 3 3 3 5 5 5 2 4 4 4 4 4 4 4 2 5 1 1 5
5 5 5 5 3 3 3 4 4 3 3 5 5 5 2 4 4 4 4 8 4 2 2 2 5 1 1 5
5 5 5 5 3 3 3 3 4 3 5 5 5 5 2 2 2 4 4 4 4 2 5 8 8 8 8 8
4 5 5 5 5 3 3 3 3 5 5 5 5 4 4 1 2 4 4 4 2 4 8 8 8 8 8 8
3 4 5 5 5 3 3 4 4 4 4 4 3 1 1 2 4 4 2 8 8 8 8 8 8 8 8 8
5 3 4 4 5 5 4 4 3 3 3 3 3 1 1 7 2 2 8 8 8 8 8 8 8 8 8 8
5 3 3 4 4 5 4 3 3 3 3 7 7 1 1 7 8 8 8 8 8 8 8 8 8 8 8 8
5 5 3 3 4 4 3 3 3 3 7 7 7 1 8 8 8 8 8 8 8 8 8 8 8 8 1 1
5 5 3 3 3 4 3 3 3 7 7 7 8 8 8 8 8 8 8 8 8 8 8 8 1 1 1 1
5 5 5 3 3 3 1 1 7 7 7 8 8 8 8 6 8 8 8 8 1 1 1 1 8 8
5 7 7 3 3 3 1 1 7 7 8 8 8 8 8 6 6 6 6 6 6 1 1 1 1 8 8 8
7 7 7 7 3 3 1 7 7 8 8 8 8 8 6 6 6 6 6 6 6 1 1 8 8 8 8 8
7 7 7 7 1 1 7 7 8 8 8 8 8 6 6 6 6 6 2 6 6 1 8 8 8 8 8 8
7 7 7 7 1 1 7 8 8 8 8 8 6 6 6 6 6 7 6 6 8 8 8 8 8 8 8 8
7 7 7 1 1 1 8 8 8 8 6 6 6 6 6 6 6 6 6 8 8 8 8 8 8 8 8 8
7 7 7 1 1 8 8 8 8 6 6 6 6 6 6 6 6 6 6 8 8 8 8 8 8 8 8 8
7 7 7 1 8 8 8 8 6 6 6 6 6 6 6 6 6 6 8 8 8 8 8 8 8 8 8 8
7 7 7 8 8 8 8 6 6 6 6 6 6 6 6 6 6 8 8 8 8 8 8 8 8 8 8 8
7 7 7 8 8 8 2 6 6 6 6 6 6 6 6 6 8 8 8 8 8 8 8 8 8 8 8 8
7 7 8 8 8 2 2 6 6 6 6 6 6 6 6 6 8 8 8 8 8 8 8 8 8 8 8 8
7 7 8 8 2 2 7 6 6 6 6 6 7 2 6 6 8 8 8 8 8 8 8 8 8 8 8 8
7 8 8 2 2 7 6 6 2 2 2 2 2 7 2 6 8 8 8 8 2 8 8 8 8 8 8 8
7 8 8 2 2 7 6 2 2 7 7 2 2 7 2 2 2 8 2 8 8 8 8 8 8 8 7 7
8 8 8 8 8 7 7 7 2 2 2 2 7 2 2 2 2 2 2 2 2 8 8 1 7 7 7
8 8 8 8 8 2 2 2 2 2 2 7 8 8 2 2 2 2 8 8 8 8 1 1 7 7 7
8 8 8 8 2 2 2 2 2 2 2 7 8 2 2 8 8 8 8 2 2 8 7 1 1 7 7 1
8 8 8 8 2 2 2 2 7 7 2 2 8 8 8 8 8 8 7 7 1 1 1 7 7 1
8 8 8 8 1 1 1 2 2 2 2 2 2 2 2 8 8 8 8 7 7 1 1 1 7 7 1
8 8 8 8 1 1 8 8 2 2 2 2 8 8 8 8 8 8 7 7 7 1 1 7 7 7 1
8 8 8 1 1 1 8 8 8 8 8 2 2 8 8 8 8 8 7 7 7 7 1 1 7 7 7 1
```

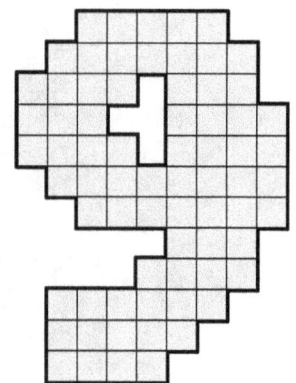

10-5-12-12-25-6-9-18-8

Suggested Colors

1	purple	PlPu
2	light blue	OVB
3	pink	PePi
4	light green	KL
5	dark blue	BSB
6	dark green	FG

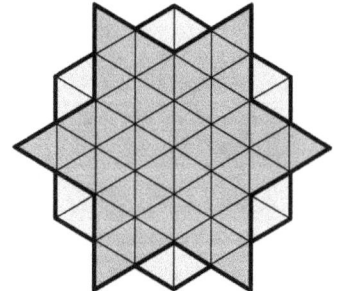

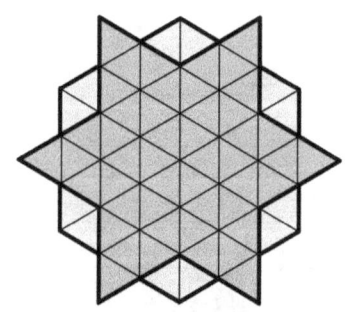

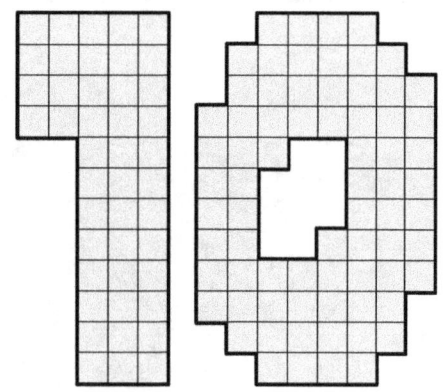

18-15-3-11

23-1-12-12-1-2-25

Suggested Colors

1 dark green   FG
2 yellow-orange   SM
3 gray   CNG
4 black   TB
5 light blue   OVB
6 brown   HB

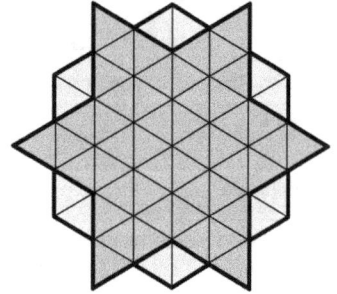
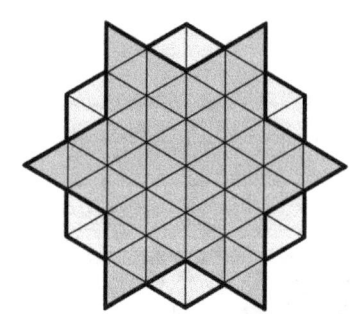

```
5 5 5 5 5 5 5 5 5 5 5 5 5 5 5 5 5 5 5 5 5 5 5 2 2 5 5 5 5
5 5 5 5 5 5 5 5 5 5 5 5 5 5 2 2 5 5 5 5 5 2 2 6 5 5 5 5
5 5 5 5 5 5 2 2 5 5 5 5 5 6 2 2 5 5 5 5 2 2 6 5 5 5 5
5 5 5 5 5 5 2 2 2 2 5 5 5 6 2 2 2 5 5 5 2 6 6 5 5 5 5
5 5 5 5 5 5 2 2 2 2 5 5 5 5 6 2 2 2 5 5 2 6 6 5 5 5 5
5 5 5 5 5 5 2 2 5 5 5 5 5 5 5 6 2 2 3 3 3 3 5 5 5 5
4 4 4 4 5 5 5 5 5 5 5 5 5 5 5 3 3 3 3 3 3 4 5 5 5 5
6 6 4 4 4 5 5 5 5 5 5 5 5 5 5 4 3 3 3 4 3 3 4 4 5 5
6 6 6 6 6 4 4 5 5 5 5 5 5 5 5 4 3 3 3 3 3 3 3 4 5 5
6 6 6 6 6 6 4 4 5 5 5 5 5 5 4 4 3 3 3 3 3 3 3 5 5
6 6 6 6 6 6 4 5 5 5 5 5 5 4 4 3 4 3 3 3 3 4 4 5 5 1
1 1 6 6 6 6 6 6 4 5 5 5 5 4 3 3 3 3 3 3 3 3 5 5 5 1 1
1 1 1 6 6 6 6 6 6 6 5 5 4 4 3 4 3 3 3 4 2 3 3 3 3 1 1 1 1
1 1 1 1 6 6 6 6 6 6 6 4 4 3 4 3 3 4 4 2 2 3 3 2 4 1 6 6
1 4 4 4 4 6 6 6 6 6 4 3 4 3 3 3 3 4 2 2 2 3 3 2 2 4 6 6
4 4 4 6 6 1 1 6 6 4 3 4 3 4 3 4 3 4 2 2 2 3 3 2 2 4 6 6
4 6 6 6 6 6 1 1 4 4 3 4 3 3 4 3 3 4 4 2 2 2 3 1 2 2 6 1
6 1 1 1 1 6 6 6 4 3 4 3 4 3 4 3 3 3 4 2 2 2 2 1 1 2 1 1
1 1 1 1 1 1 6 4 4 3 4 3 3 3 3 3 3 3 4 2 2 2 2 4 4 1 1
1 1 1 1 1 1 6 4 4 3 3 3 4 3 3 3 3 3 3 3 2 2 2 4 1 1
1 1 1 1 1 1 1 4 3 4 3 4 3 4 3 3 3 3 3 3 1 4 4 1 1 1
4 4 4 1 1 1 1 4 3 4 3 3 3 4 3 2 2 3 3 3 3 4 1 1 4 1 1 1
4 4 4 4 1 1 4 4 3 4 3 3 4 3 2 2 3 3 4 2 2 2 1 2 2 2 1
6 6 4 4 4 1 1 4 3 4 3 4 3 4 3 4 2 2 3 4 2 6 2 1 2 6 2 1
6 4 6 6 4 4 1 4 3 4 3 3 3 3 4 3 4 2 2 3 4 2 6 3 3 3 3 2 1
4 4 6 4 6 4 1 4 4 3 4 3 4 3 4 3 3 2 3 4 4 3 4 3 3 3 4 1 1
4 6 6 6 6 6 4 4 3 4 3 4 3 4 3 3 3 2 3 4 4 3 3 3 3 3 1 1
6 6 6 6 6 6 6 4 3 4 3 4 3 4 3 4 3 2 3 4 3 3 4 4 3 1 1
6 6 6 6 6 6 6 4 3 4 3 3 3 4 3 3 2 2 3 3 4 3 3 3 1 1 1
1 1 6 1 1 6 6 6 4 3 4 3 4 3 4 3 4 2 2 3 3 3 3 1 1 1 1 1 1
1 1 1 1 1 1 6 6 4 4 3 4 3 3 3 4 2 3 3 3 3 3 1 1 1 1 6 6
1 1 1 1 1 1 1 1 1 4 6 3 3 4 3 3 2 2 3 3 3 3 1 1 1 6 6 6
1 1 1 1 1 1 1 1 6 2 2 3 4 3 2 2 3 3 3 3 1 1 1 1 1 1 1
1 1 1 1 1 1 1 4 6 2 2 2 3 3 2 2 2 2 6 6 6 4 4 1 1 1 1
1 1 1 1 1 1 4 6 6 2 2 1 1 2 2 2 6 6 6 4 4 4 4 1 1 1
1 1 1 1 1 4 6 6 6 6 1 1 1 3 3 3 3 3 3 3 3 3 3 3 3 3
1 1 1 1 1 4 2 2 6 6 1 1 1 3 3 3 3 3 3 3 3 3 3 3 4 4
1 1 1 4 6 6 2 2 2 1 1 1 1 3 3 3 3 3 3 4 4 4 4 4 3 3
4 6 6 2 6 6 6 2 1 1 3 3 3 4 4 4 4 4 4 4 3 3 3 3 3 3
6 6 2 2 2 6 6 1 1 3 3 3 3 3 3 3 3 3 3 3 3 3 3 3 3 3
```

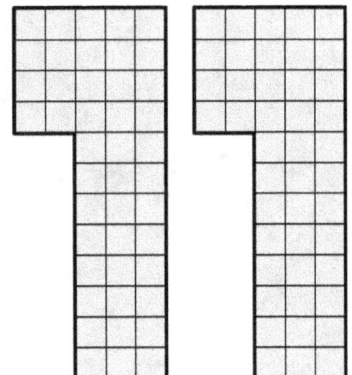

1-12-12-9-7-1-20-15-18

Suggested Colors

1	dark green	FG
2	black	TB
3	gray	CNG
4	dark blue	MB
5	light brown	THT

Back-up Colors

1 green
2 black
3 brown
4 blue
5 orange

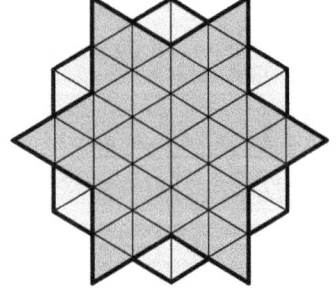 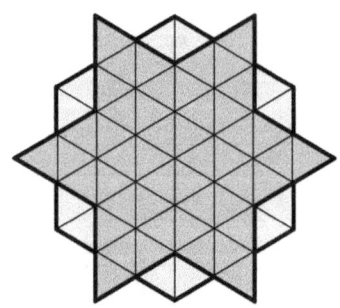

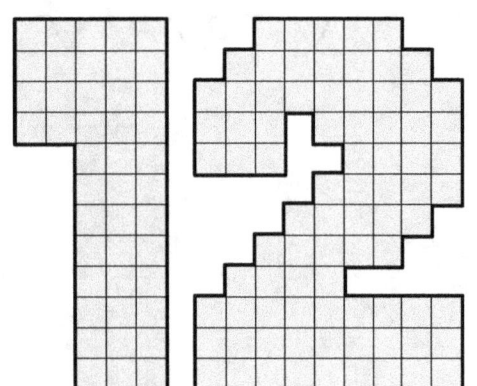

Suggested Colors

1	orange	SO
2	yellow	YB
3	red	RR
4	light gray	CNG
5	dark brown	WB
6	light blue	OVB
7	dark purple	PlPu
8	light brown	THT

Back-up Colors

1	orange
2	yellow
3	red
4	brown
5	black
6	blue
7	purple
8	green

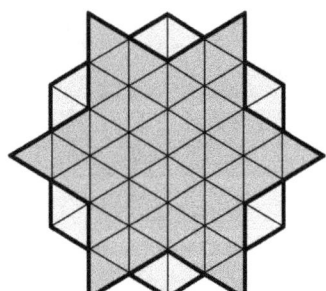

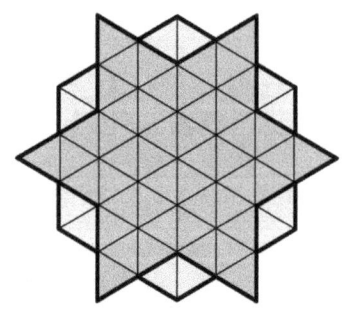

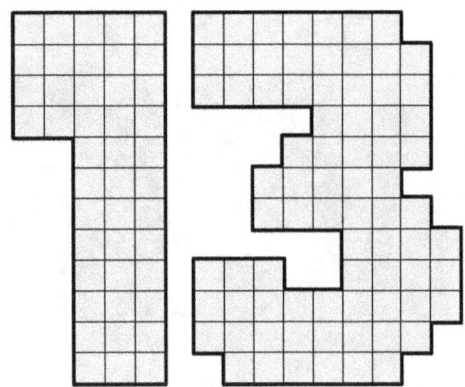

2-21-12-12-8-5-1-4

19-8-1-18-11

Suggested Colors

1	yellow-orange	SM
2	light brown	THT
3	black	TB
4	dark magenta pink	FP
5	dark brown	WB
6	dark green	KL

Back-up Colors

1	yellow (or leave white)
2	gray or orange
3	black
4	red
5	brown
6	green

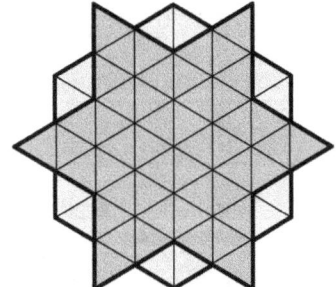
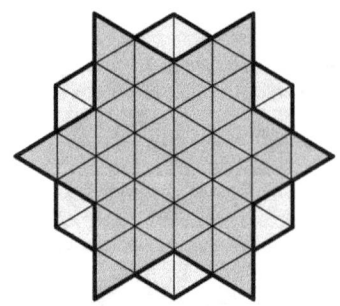
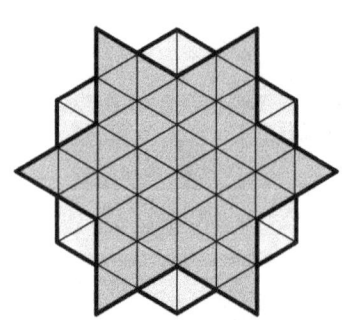

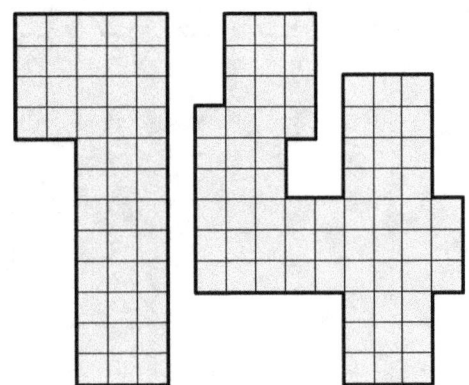

8-21-13-13-9-14-7-2-9-18-4

Suggested Colors

1	dark blue	BSB
2	dark green	FG
3	black	TB
4	yellow	YB
5	brown	HB
6	red	SO
7	light green	MG
8	light blue	OVB

Back-up Colors

1	purple
2	green
3	black
4	orange
5	brown
6	red
7	yellow
8	blue

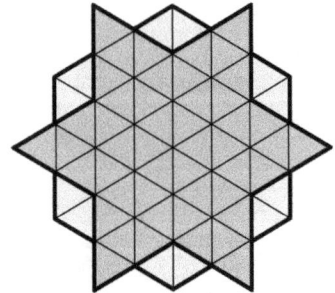
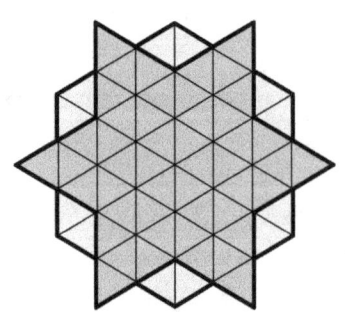
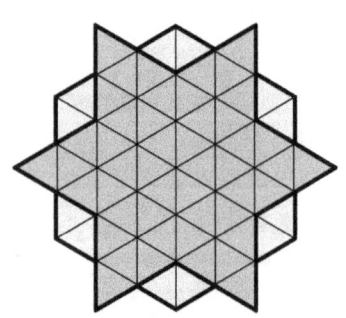

```
1 1 1 7 2 1 1 1 1 5 6 6 6 6 6 1 5 6 6 6 1 5 6 6 6 6 1 4 1 1 1
1 7 7 7 2 1 1 1 1 1 5 6 6 6 6 5 6 6 6 5 6 6 6 6 1 1 4 1 4 4
7 7 7 2 2 4 4 1 1 1 8 5 6 6 6 1 5 5 5 6 6 1 1 6 6 4 4 1
7 7 2 2 2 1 4 4 1 8 1 8 5 6 7 7 2 2 7 7 2 8 6 6 6 6 1 1
7 7 2 2 1 8 4 6 6 6 6 6 1 1 7 7 2 7 7 2 8 6 6 6 5 5 4 4
7 2 2 1 4 4 6 6 6 6 6 6 7 2 7 7 7 2 7 2 6 5 5 8 1 8 1
2 2 1 1 8 8 4 6 6 6 6 6 5 7 7 7 7 7 7 7 7 7 7 7 7 1 8
5 5 5 8 1 4 4 6 6 5 5 5 8 5 5 7 7 2 7 7 7 7 7 7 7 7 7
3 5 5 5 8 7 7 7 7 2 2 8 6 6 7 7 2 2 2 2 7 7 1 1 7 7 7
1 3 5 5 7 7 7 7 2 2 8 6 6 6 2 2 1 2 2 2 2 6 6 6 8 1 7 7
7 3 5 7 7 7 2 2 2 8 6 6 6 6 6 5 1 8 5 5 8 2 6 6 6 6 8 8 1
7 3 5 2 2 2 2 8 6 6 6 6 6 5 8 5 6 5 1 8 5 6 6 6 6 1 8
2 3 5 5 8 1 1 8 6 6 6 6 6 5 8 1 5 6 6 8 1 8 5 6 6 6 6 8
2 3 5 5 1 4 4 6 6 6 6 6 5 8 1 8 6 6 6 8 8 8 5 6 6 6 6 4
8 3 5 5 1 8 4 6 6 6 6 6 5 8 8 8 6 4 6 8 8 1 8 5 6 6 4 8
1 3 5 5 8 1 8 4 6 6 6 5 8 1 8 8 4 4 8 8 8 8 8 4 4 8 4
7 8 3 5 5 8 4 4 4 6 4 8 8 8 8 8 4 8 4 8 1 8 8 8 4 8 8 8
7 7 3 5 5 8 4 1 4 8 4 1 8 8 1 8 8 8 8 8 8 1 8 8 8 8 8 8
2 7 3 5 5 8 8 8 8 8 8 8 8 8 8 8 8 1 8 8 8 8 8 8 8 8 1 8
2 2 2 3 5 5 3 3 3 3 3 8 8 8 8 8 8 8 8 8 8 8 8 8 8 8 8
2 2 2 3 5 5 8 3 3 3 3 3 3 8 8 8 8 8 8 3 1 1 1 8 8 8 8
2 2 8 3 5 5 8 8 8 3 3 3 3 3 8 8 8 8 3 1 3 1 3 3 3 3 3
8 8 3 3 3 3 3 3 3 3 3 2 2 2 2 3 8 3 1 1 1 1 3 3 8 8 8
8 3 3 1 1 1 1 1 1 1 3 3 1 3 2 2 2 3 3 1 1 1 1 1 8 8 7 8
8 8 8 3 3 3 3 3 3 3 1 1 3 3 1 3 2 2 2 2 3 1 1 8 8 8 7 7
7 7 8 5 5 3 3 1 1 1 3 3 3 1 3 1 3 2 2 2 2 2 3 8 8 8 2 7
7 7 7 3 5 5 5 8 3 3 3 1 1 3 3 1 3 2 7 2 2 2 8 8 7 8 2 2
2 7 7 7 3 5 5 8 8 7 1 1 3 3 1 3 4 2 4 7 2 2 8 7 7 8 2 2
2 7 7 7 3 5 5 5 7 7 7 7 8 1 3 4 2 4 7 2 7 2 8 7 7 7 8 2
2 2 7 7 7 3 5 5 7 7 7 2 8 8 2 4 4 4 4 7 2 8 2 7 7 7 8 8
2 2 2 7 7 3 5 5 7 2 2 2 8 8 2 7 4 4 7 4 7 8 2 7 7 7 8 8
8 2 2 2 7 3 5 5 2 2 2 8 8 3 5 4 4 3 4 3 8 8 2 7 7 7 8 5
8 8 2 2 7 3 5 5 2 2 8 8 3 5 5 5 4 3 4 3 8 8 2 2 7 7 5 5
8 8 8 8 3 5 5 5 8 8 8 3 5 5 3 5 6 4 4 4 8 8 2 2 2 7 5 5
8 8 8 8 3 5 5 5 8 8 8 3 5 3 3 5 6 6 5 6 8 8 8 2 2 5 5 5
8 7 7 7 3 5 5 8 8 8 8 3 3 3 5 5 5 6 6 6 8 8 8 8 5 5 5 3
7 7 7 7 3 5 5 7 7 7 8 3 8 3 5 3 6 5 6 5 5 6 8 8 8 5 5 3 8
7 7 7 2 3 5 5 7 7 7 7 8 3 5 3 6 5 6 6 5 6 6 8 5 5 3 8
7 7 2 2 3 5 5 2 2 2 7 7 8 3 5 5 6 5 6 5 5 6 8 5 5 3 7 7
2 2 2 8 3 5 5 8 2 2 2 2 2 3 5 8 6 8 6 6 6 8 8 5 5 5 3 2 2
```

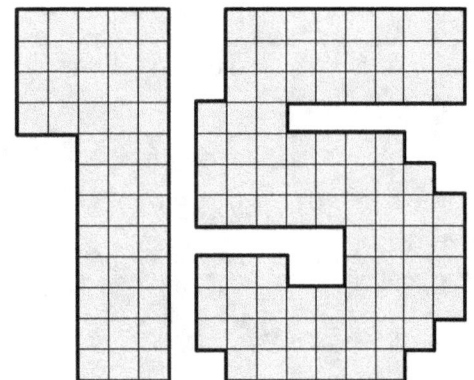

5-12-5-16-8-1-14-20

Suggested Colors

1	yellow-orange	MG
2	yellow	YB
3	gray	CNG
4	light pink	PePi
5	blue	BSB
6	black	TB
7	light green	MG
8	brown	HB

Back-up Colors

1	red
2	yellow
3	gray or brown
4	purple
5	blue
6	black
7	green
8	orange

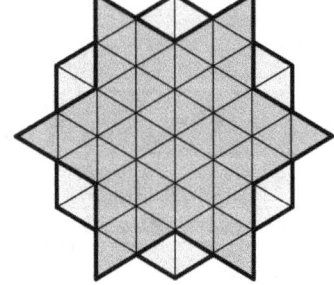
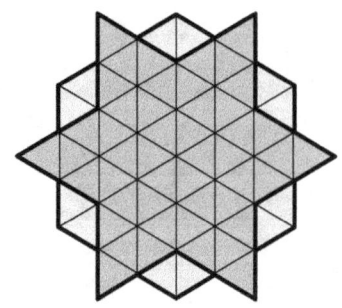
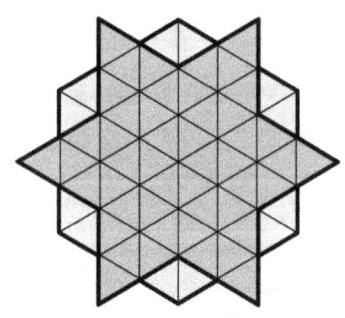

```
6 6 6 6 6 6 6 5 5 5 5 5 5 5 5 5 5 5 5 5 5 5 5 5 5 5 5 5 5 5 5 5 5 5
6 6 6 6 6 6 6 6 5 5 6 6 5 6 6 5 5 5 5 5 5 5 5 5 5 5 5 5 5 5 5 5 5 5
6 6 6 6 6 6 6 6 6 5 5 5 6 6 5 5 5 5 5 5 5 5 6 5 6 6 5 5 5
8 8 8 8 8 8 8 8 5 5 5 5 5 5 5 5 5 5 5 5 5 5 5 6 6 5 5 5 3
8 8 8 8 8 8 8 8 8 3 3 3 5 5 5 3 3 3 3 5 5 5 5 5 3 3 3
6 6 8 8 6 6 8 3 3 3 3 3 3 3 3 3 3 3 3 3 5 5 3 3 3 3 3
6 6 8 8 6 6 3 6 3 3 3 3 6 3 6 3 3 6 3 6 3 6 3 3 3 3 3
6 6 8 8 6 3 6 3 3 3 3 6 3 6 3 3 3 6 3 6 6 6 6 6 3 3 3
8 8 8 8 6 6 3 6 3 3 3 6 3 3 3 6 3 6 6 6 6 6 6 6 3 3
8 8 8 8 3 3 6 3 3 3 6 3 3 3 6 3 6 6 6 3 6 3 3 6 6 6
8 8 8 8 6 3 3 3 3 6 3 6 3 3 3 6 6 6 3 6 3 3 3 3 6
6 6 6 6 6 3 3 3 3 3 1 3 3 3 3 3 3 3 6 3 6 3 3 1 3 3 1 3
8 8 8 8 3 4 4 3 3 1 1 1 3 3 4 4 3 3 3 3 3 1 3 1 3 3
6 6 8 8 3 3 2 4 1 1 2 1 1 4 2 3 3 3 3 3 3 1 1 1 3 1
6 6 8 8 3 4 4 3 3 1 1 1 3 3 4 4 3 3 3 3 3 3 1 1 1 3
6 6 8 6 3 6 3 3 3 7 1 7 3 3 3 3 6 3 6 3 3 3 4 4 3 3 3
8 8 8 6 6 6 3 7 7 7 7 7 3 6 6 6 3 3 3 4 4 4 4 3 3
8 8 8 8 3 8 6 3 7 7 2 7 7 3 6 8 3 3 3 4 4 2 4 4 3 3
8 8 8 8 3 3 3 3 7 3 2 7 7 3 3 3 3 3 3 7 3 4 2 2 4 6 6
6 6 6 6 6 3 3 3 4 4 4 3 3 3 1 3 3 7 2 7 3 3 2 3 6 3
8 8 8 8 8 3 6 3 3 4 4 4 4 3 1 2 1 3 3 7 3 3 3 3 6 6 3 3
6 6 8 8 6 6 3 3 4 4 2 4 4 6 3 3 3 4 3 3 6 6 3 6 3 3 1 1
6 6 8 8 6 6 3 6 4 4 2 4 4 6 3 3 3 4 3 3 6 6 6 3 7 7 1 1
6 6 8 8 6 3 6 3 4 3 3 4 3 3 3 3 4 7 4 3 6 7 1 1 7 7 7 1
8 8 8 8 8 3 3 3 7 7 3 3 6 3 3 3 4 3 6 6 7 1 1 1 7 7 3
8 8 8 8 8 3 6 7 7 7 7 7 3 3 3 3 6 6 6 3 6 7 1 1 1 4 4 3
8 8 8 8 8 8 3 7 7 2 7 7 3 3 6 6 3 3 6 6 4 3 3 4 4
6 6 6 6 6 6 3 7 7 2 7 7 3 6 6 6 6 3 3 3 3 3 4 3 3 3
1 1 1 1 1 1 3 7 3 3 7 3 3 6 6 6 6 3 3 3 3 6 3 4 4 3 7
6 1 6 6 1 6 1 3 3 3 3 3 3 6 6 6 6 3 3 6 3 3 3 3 7 1
8 8 8 8 8 8 3 3 3 7 3 1 3 6 6 6 3 3 3 3 6 3 3 3 3 7
8 8 6 6 6 8 8 1 7 7 7 1 3 3 6 6 3 3 3 3 6 2 3 3 3 4 3
8 8 6 6 6 8 8 1 1 7 1 1 2 3 3 3 3 4 6 1 2 3 4 2 4 3
8 8 6 6 6 8 8 6 1 1 1 2 2 4 3 3 3 2 4 6 1 2 1 3 4 3
8 8 6 6 6 8 8 3 6 1 2 2 4 4 7 3 1 2 6 2 2 1 1 3 3 3 3
8 8 3 3 3 8 8 3 2 6 2 4 4 7 7 1 1 6 1 1 1 1 2 2 3 3 1
6 6 6 6 6 6 6 6 3 2 2 6 4 7 7 1 1 6 2 2 2 2 2 3 3 1 7
6 3 6 6 6 3 6 3 7 7 2 2 6 6 6 6 6 7 7 7 7 7 7 7 3 3 1
3 6 6 3 3 6 6 7 7 7 7 7 3 6 6 6 7 3 6 6 7 7 7 7 3 3
3 3 6 3 6 3 6 7 7 7 3 3 7 7 7 6 6 6 6 7 3 3 3 3 7 7 7 3 3
```

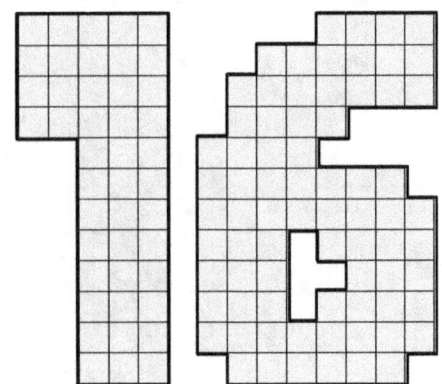

2-21-20-20-5-18-6-12-9-5-19

Suggested Colors

1 brown   WB
2 light blue   OVB
3 yellow   YB
4 dark magenta pink   FP
5 black   TB
6 yellow-orange   SM
7 red   RR
8 light green   KL

Back-up Colors

1 brown
2 blue
3 yellow
4 red
5 black
6 orange
7 purple
8 green

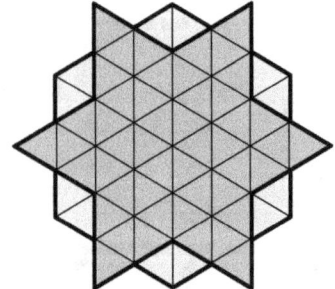
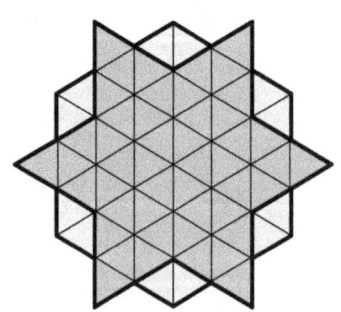
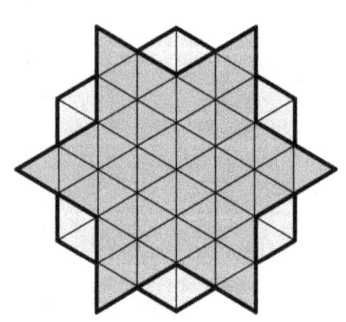

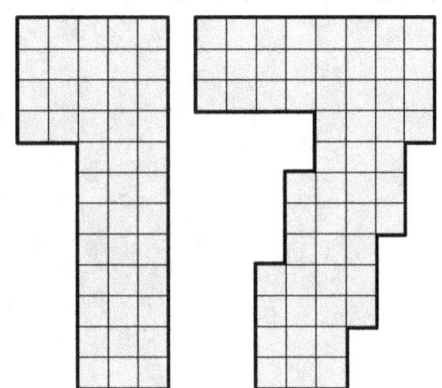

3-8-1-13-5-12-5-15-14

Suggested Colors

1	red	RR
2	dark brown	WB
3	light blue	OVB
4	midnight blue	DSB
5	blue-green	HA
6	dark green	KL
7	yellow	YB

Back-up Colors

1	red
2	brown
3	blue
4	black
5	purple
6	green
7	yellow

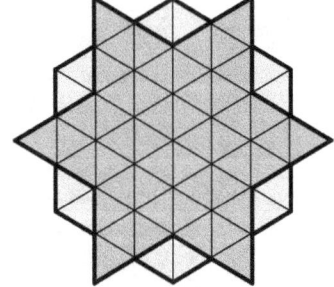
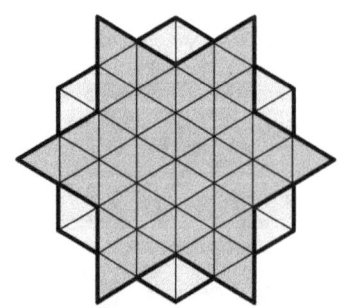
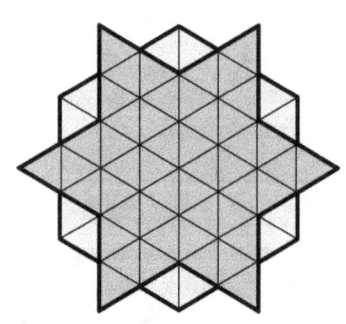

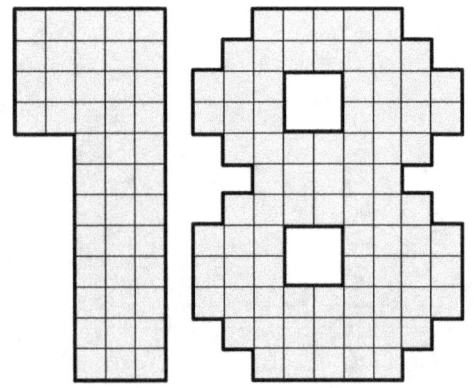

15-23-12-19

Suggested Colors

1	dark green	FG
2	gray	CNG
3	light green	MG
4	yellow	YB
5	brown	HB
6	yellow-orange	SM
7	black	TB

Back-up Colors

1	green
2	gray or red
3	blue
4	yellow
5	brown
6	light brown or orange
7	black

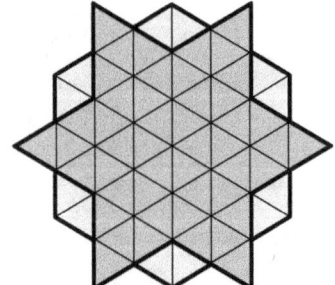 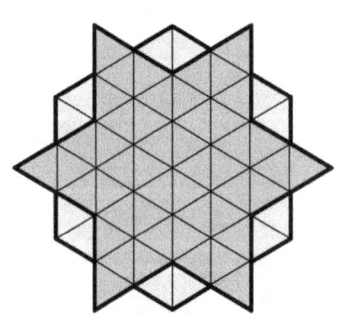 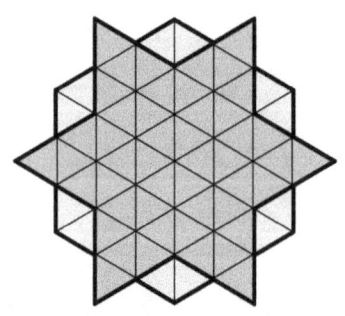

```
3 3 3 3 3 1 1 1 1 3 3 3 3 3 3 3 3 3 3 1 3 5 3 1 1 1 3 3
3 3 3 3 3 3 1 1 2 2 2 2 2 3 3 3 3 3 1 1 3 5 3 1 1 3 3 5
3 1 1 1 3 3 3 2 5 5 5 5 2 2 2 2 3 3 1 1 3 3 5 3 3 3 5 5
1 1 1 1 1 3 2 5 5 2 4 5 5 2 5 5 2 3 1 1 1 3 5 3 3 5 5 3
1 1 1 3 3 3 2 5 2 4 7 4 5 5 4 5 5 3 1 1 1 3 5 3 5 5 3 3
1 1 3 3 3 3 2 5 2 2 4 2 2 4 7 4 5 3 3 1 1 5 5 5 5 3 3 3
3 3 3 3 3 3 2 5 5 2 2 2 7 2 4 2 5 3 3 3 3 5 5 3 3 3 1 1
3 3 3 3 3 5 2 2 5 5 2 2 7 2 2 5 5 3 3 3 5 5 3 1 1 1 1 1
3 3 3 3 5 5 2 5 5 2 2 2 2 2 5 5 2 3 3 5 5 3 1 1 1 1 1 3
1 3 3 5 2 5 5 2 2 2 2 2 2 2 5 2 3 3 3 5 5 3 3 1 1 1 3 3
1 1 3 5 5 2 2 2 5 2 2 2 2 2 3 3 6 6 6 6 6 6 3 3 3 3 3 3
1 1 5 2 5 2 2 5 2 2 5 2 2 5 3 3 6 5 5 6 5 5 5 6 3 3 1 3
1 1 5 5 2 2 2 2 2 5 2 2 5 2 3 3 6 6 6 5 5 6 5 5 6 3 1 1
1 5 2 5 2 5 2 2 2 2 2 2 2 3 6 5 5 6 5 6 4 6 5 5 3 1 1
1 5 5 2 2 5 2 2 5 2 2 5 2 2 3 6 6 6 6 5 4 7 4 6 5 3 3 1
1 2 5 2 5 2 2 5 2 2 5 2 2 3 5 5 6 6 5 6 4 6 6 6 3 3 3
1 5 2 2 2 2 5 2 2 5 2 2 3 3 6 6 6 6 5 6 6 6 7 6 3 3 3
1 2 2 5 2 2 2 2 2 2 2 3 3 6 5 6 6 6 5 6 6 7 6 3 3 1
5 2 2 5 2 2 5 2 2 5 2 2 3 6 5 6 6 6 5 5 6 6 6 3 3 1 1
5 6 2 2 2 5 2 2 5 2 2 3 3 6 5 6 5 6 5 6 6 5 5 5 5 1 1
6 6 6 6 2 5 2 2 5 2 2 2 3 3 6 6 6 6 6 6 6 6 6 5 5 5 5 1
5 5 6 5 6 2 2 2 2 2 3 3 6 6 6 5 6 5 6 6 6 6 5 5
2 5 7 5 6 5 2 6 2 2 3 3 3 1 6 5 6 5 5 6 6 6 5 6 6 5 6 5
2 2 5 5 7 5 6 6 6 3 3 1 1 1 6 5 6 6 5 5 5 6 6 6 6 6 5 6
2 2 2 5 5 5 6 5 6 6 1 1 1 1 6 6 6 6 5 2 5 5 6 6 5 6 6 6
2 5 2 2 5 5 7 5 6 5 6 1 1 3 3 6 5 6 5 2 5 2 5 6 6 5 6 6
5 2 2 5 2 5 5 5 7 5 7 5 3 3 3 6 5 6 5 2 5 2 5 5 6 6 6 6
2 2 5 2 2 2 5 2 5 5 5 5 5 3 3 6 6 6 5 2 5 2 5 2 5 5 5 6
3 3 2 2 2 3 3 5 5 5 5 5 5 6 6 6 6 6 5 5 2 5 2 5 2 5 5 5
3 3 3 3 3 3 3 3 5 5 2 5 5 6 6 6 5 5 6 6 6 5 2 5 2 5 2 5 2
1 1 3 3 3 3 3 3 5 5 2 7 5 6 5 6 5 5 6 6 6 5 2 5 2 5 2 5 2
1 1 1 3 3 1 1 1 3 3 5 5 5 6 5 7 5 5 5 6 6 5 5 2 5 2 5 2
1 1 1 3 3 1 1 3 3 3 5 5 7 5 5 5 2 5 5 6 6 5 5 2 5 2 5 2
3 1 1 5 5 3 3 3 3 5 5 5 5 5 5 2 2 5 5 6 6 5 5 6 6 5 5 2
3 3 3 3 5 5 5 5 5 5 5 2 2 5 2 5 5 6 6 6 6 6 5 5 6 6 6 5
5 5 5 5 5 5 5 5 2 2 5 5 5 5 5 5 7 5 5 6 5 5 7 5 5 6 6 6
5 2 2 2 5 2 5 5 5 5 5 5 5 5 5 5 5 5 5 6 5 5 5 5 5 6 5 6
5 5 5 5 5 5 5 5 5 5 5 5 2 2 5 5 2 2 5 7 5 2 2 5 5 6 5 6
2 2 5 5 5 5 5 5 5 2 2 2 5 5 5 5 5 5 5 5 5 5 5 5 3 3 6 3
5 5 5 2 5 2 2 2 5 5 5 5 5 5 2 2 2 5 3 3 3 3 3 3 3 3 6 6
```

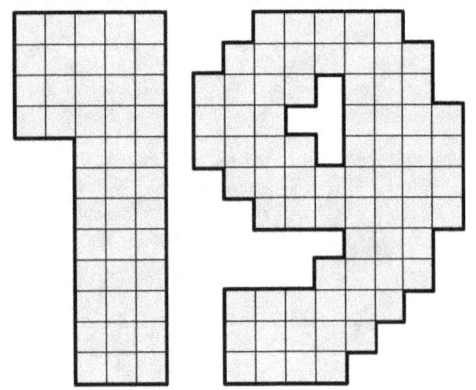

19-5-1

20-21-18-20-12-5

Suggested Colors

1	dark green	KL
2	black	TB
3	dark brown	WB
4	red-orange	SO
5	blue-green	HA
6	gray	CNG

Back-up Colors

1	green
2	black
3	brown
4	red
5	blue
6	gray or orange

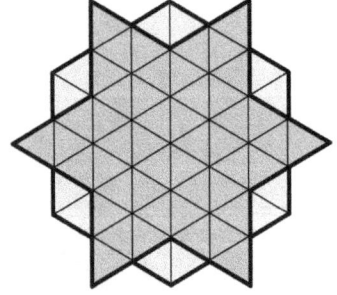 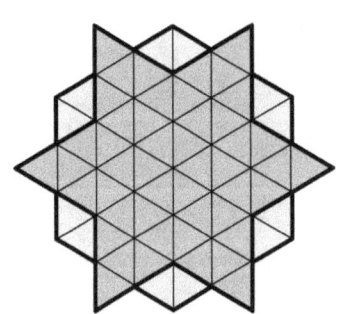 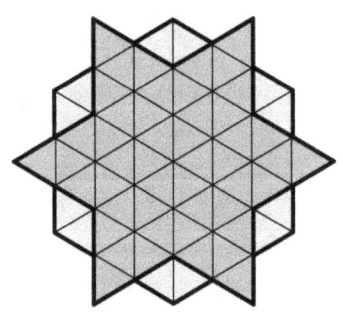

5	5	5	5	5	5	5	5	5	5	5	5	5	5	5	5	5	5	5	5	5	5	5	5	5	5	5	5
5	6	5	5	5	5	5	5	5	5	5	5	5	5	5	5	5	5	5	5	5	5	5	5	6	5	5	5
5	5	5	5	5	5	5	5	5	5	6	5	5	5	5	5	6	5	5	5	5	5	5	5	5	5	5	5
5	5	5	5	5	5	5	5	5	5	5	5	5	5	5	5	5	5	5	5	2	5	5	5	5	5	5	5
5	5	5	6	5	5	5	5	5	5	5	5	5	5	5	5	5	5	5	2	3	5	5	5	5	5	5	5
5	5	5	5	5	5	5	5	5	5	5	5	5	6	5	5	5	5	5	2	3	5	5	5	5	5	5	5
5	5	5	5	5	5	5	5	6	5	5	5	5	5	5	5	2	2	2	2	2	2	2	2	5	5	5	5
6	5	5	5	5	5	5	5	5	5	5	6	5	5	2	2	2	3	3	2	3	3	2	2	5	3	2	3
5	5	5	5	6	5	6	5	5	5	5	5	2	2	2	4	3	2	2	3	3	2	2	2	2	3	2	3
5	5	6	5	5	5	5	5	6	5	2	2	2	4	3	2	2	2	4	2	2	2	2	2	2	3	3	2
6	5	5	5	1	5	5	5	5	2	2	3	2	2	2	2	2	4	3	2	4	3	3	2	2	2	2	5
5	1	5	5	1	5	6	5	2	3	4	4	3	2	3	4	2	2	2	2	2	4	4	2	2	5	5	6
5	1	5	1	5	5	5	2	2	2	3	3	3	2	4	3	4	2	3	3	3	2	2	2	3	5	5	5
6	1	6	1	5	5	2	2	3	2	2	2	2	2	4	4	3	2	3	4	4	4	3	2	2	5	6	5
6	1	6	1	6	6	2	3	4	3	2	3	4	2	2	2	2	2	2	3	4	3	4	2	3	5	5	5
6	1	6	6	6	6	2	4	4	3	2	4	3	4	2	3	3	3	2	4	2	4	2	2	2	5	1	5
6	6	6	6	6	6	2	3	3	2	2	2	4	3	2	3	3	3	4	3	2	2	2	3	3	5	1	5
2	2	3	2	6	6	2	2	2	4	3	2	2	2	2	2	2	4	3	4	3	2	3	4	6	6	1	6
3	3	2	2	3	2	2	2	4	3	3	3	2	4	3	3	2	2	4	4	2	3	3	6	6	6	1	6
2	3	3	3	2	2	3	2	2	3	3	4	2	3	4	4	4	2	2	2	3	4	6	6	6	6	6	1
6	2	3	3	3	3	3	2	2	2	4	2	2	3	4	3	3	2	3	4	3	6	6	6	1	6	6	1
6	6	2	2	2	2	4	3	3	2	2	2	2	2	2	2	2	4	3	6	6	1	6	6	1	6	1	1
6	6	6	6	6	6	3	4	4	3	2	2	2	2	4	3	3	6	6	6	6	1	6	1	6	6	1	6
6	6	6	6	3	4	2	3	4	4	4	3	2	3	2	2	6	6	6	6	6	1	6	1	6	6	1	6
6	6	6	3	4	2	3	4	3	4	6	6	6	2	3	2	2	3	2	2	6	1	6	1	6	3	6	6
6	6	3	4	2	3	4	3	4	6	6	6	6	2	2	3	3	2	2	3	2	2	6	6	6	6	6	6
6	6	3	4	3	4	2	4	4	6	6	6	6	6	2	2	3	3	3	2	2	2	3	2	6	6	6	6
3	6	3	3	4	2	2	4	6	6	6	6	6	6	6	2	2	3	3	3	3	3	2	2	3	2	2	6
6	6	3	3	4	4	4	6	6	1	6	6	6	6	6	6	6	2	2	2	2	2	3	3	2	2	6	6
6	6	6	3	4	6	6	6	6	1	6	3	6	6	6	6	6	6	6	6	6	6	6	6	6	6	6	6
1	6	6	6	6	6	6	1	6	1	6	6	6	1	6	6	6	6	6	6	6	6	6	6	6	1	6	6
1	6	6	3	6	6	6	1	6	1	1	6	6	1	6	6	6	6	6	3	6	6	6	6	6	1	6	3
1	6	6	6	6	6	6	1	6	6	1	6	6	1	6	3	6	6	6	6	6	6	3	6	6	1	1	6
1	6	6	6	1	6	6	6	6	6	1	6	1	6	6	6	6	6	6	6	6	6	6	6	6	6	1	6
1	6	6	6	1	6	3	6	1	6	1	6	1	6	3	6	6	3	6	6	6	6	6	6	1	6	1	6
6	3	6	6	1	1	6	6	1	6	6	6	1	6	6	1	6	6	6	6	6	3	6	6	1	6	6	6
6	6	6	6	6	1	6	6	1	6	3	6	6	6	6	1	6	6	6	6	6	6	6	6	1	6	6	6
6	6	3	6	6	6	6	6	1	6	6	1	6	3	1	1	6	6	6	3	6	6	6	6	1	6	3	6
3	6	6	6	3	6	1	3	6	6	6	1	6	6	1	6	3	6	6	6	6	3	6	6	6	6	6	6
6	6	3	6	6	6	1	6	6	3	6	1	6	6	1	6	6	6	3	6	6	6	6	6	3	6	6	3

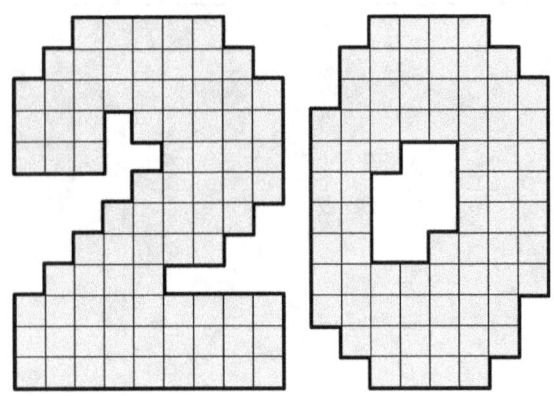

19-20-1-18-12-9-14-8

Suggested Colors

1	black	TB
2	honey brown	HB
3	yellow	YB
4	dark green	FG
5	royal blue	BSB
6	violet-red	DR
7	light blue	OVB

Back-up Colors

1	black
2	brown
3	red
4	green
5	blue
6	purple
7	yellow

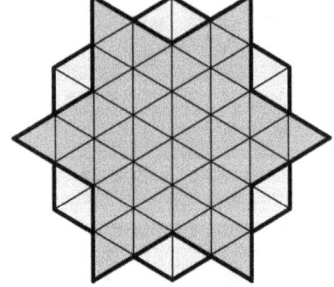 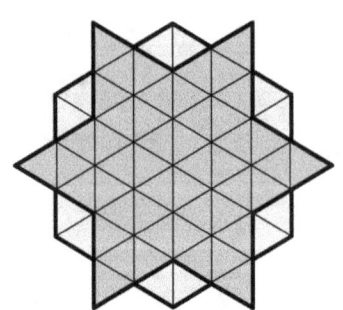 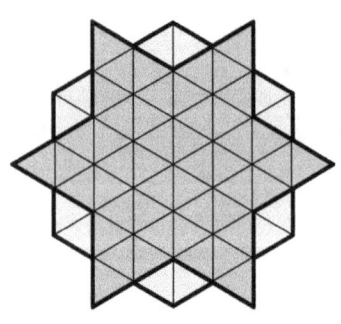

```
4 7 7 4 4 2 4 4 7 7 7 7 4 4 7 7 7 7 7 7 7 4 4 7 4 4 4 4
4 4 7 7 4 2 4 4 4 7 7 4 4 4 7 7 6 6 6 7 7 7 4 7 4 7 4 4 4
4 4 4 7 7 2 4 4 4 4 7 4 4 7 7 6 6 6 6 6 6 7 7 7 7 4 4 4
4 4 4 4 2 2 7 7 7 2 2 4 7 7 6 5 5 6 1 2 6 6 1 7 7 7 4 4
7 4 4 4 2 7 7 4 7 7 2 2 2 5 5 6 5 5 1 1 5 1 1 1 1 7 7 2
7 7 4 4 2 5 3 4 7 4 4 4 7 6 5 5 6 5 5 5 1 1 1 1 1 1 7 2
7 7 5 3 2 3 3 4 7 4 4 7 5 5 6 6 6 5 5 5 5 7 4 4 4 4 7 2
7 7 3 3 2 4 4 7 7 4 4 7 6 5 5 6 6 5 5 5 7 7 7 4 4 4 4 2
7 7 7 2 2 3 5 7 7 4 7 7 5 6 6 6 6 6 6 6 5 7 7 7 4 4 4 4
7 5 3 2 2 3 3 7 7 7 7 7 5 5 6 5 5 5 6 5 6 7 7 7 7 4 4 4
7 3 3 2 7 7 7 7 7 7 7 5 6 6 6 6 6 5 5 5 5 7 4 7 4 4 4 4
4 7 7 2 5 3 4 4 7 7 5 6 6 5 5 6 5 6 6 6 6 5 4 4 7 4 4 4
4 4 7 2 3 3 4 7 7 5 6 6 6 6 6 6 6 5 5 6 5 6 6 4 4 7 2 4 4
4 3 5 2 4 4 7 7 6 6 5 5 6 5 5 6 6 6 5 5 6 7 4 2 2 7 4
7 3 3 2 7 7 7 7 5 6 6 6 6 6 6 6 5 6 6 6 5 5 7 7 2 7 7 2
7 7 2 2 5 3 7 7 6 6 5 5 6 6 5 6 5 5 5 6 6 6 7 7 2 7 7 2
7 7 2 2 3 3 4 5 6 6 6 6 6 6 6 5 5 6 6 5 5 5 6 5 7 2 2 7 7 2
2 7 2 4 4 4 4 5 5 6 6 6 5 5 6 6 6 5 6 6 6 6 4 7 2 7 3 5 2
2 2 7 4 4 4 6 6 6 6 6 6 6 5 6 5 5 5 6 5 4 4 2 7 3 3 2
2 2 2 7 7 7 5 6 6 5 5 6 6 5 5 6 6 5 5 6 4 4 2 7 4 2 2
2 2 2 2 2 7 5 5 6 6 6 6 6 6 5 6 5 5 7 7 2 2 4 4 2 4
1 2 2 2 2 2 6 6 6 6 6 5 5 6 6 5 5 6 6 7 7 2 2 7 7 2 4
1 1 1 2 2 2 6 5 5 6 6 6 6 5 6 5 5 5 7 7 2 2 4 4 7 2 7
4 2 1 1 2 2 2 6 6 6 6 6 6 6 5 5 6 5 5 7 7 2 2 4 4 4 4 3
4 2 7 1 1 2 6 5 5 6 5 5 6 6 6 5 6 7 7 3 5 2 4 4 4 4 4
7 2 7 7 1 1 6 6 6 6 6 6 6 5 5 6 5 5 7 7 3 3 7 3 4 4 4 4
7 2 7 7 7 7 6 6 6 5 5 6 6 6 5 5 5 2 7 7 2 2 7 3 3 4 4 4
4 4 4 7 7 5 6 5 6 6 6 5 5 6 6 2 2 2 3 3 2 7 7 7 2 4 4
4 4 4 4 7 5 5 5 6 6 2 5 5 5 5 2 2 2 5 3 2 3 3 2 2 7 4
7 4 4 4 7 6 6 5 5 6 1 5 5 5 2 2 2 2 2 2 3 5 2 3 5 7
7 2 4 4 7 6 6 6 6 7 5 5 5 1 2 3 5 2 2 2 2 2 2 3 3 7
3 2 7 4 4 6 6 6 6 6 7 5 5 5 1 1 3 3 2 2 2 3 5 2 2 7 7 7
3 2 3 5 7 6 6 6 6 6 7 5 5 7 4 4 4 1 3 5 2 3 3 2 2 7 7
2 2 3 3 6 6 6 6 6 6 7 5 7 7 7 4 4 4 3 3 1 2 2 2 2 2 7
2 2 2 2 6 6 6 6 6 6 7 7 7 7 5 3 4 4 2 2 1 1 5 3 2 2 3 5
3 5 2 6 6 6 2 6 6 6 2 2 7 7 3 3 2 3 5 2 7 1 3 3 2 2 3 3
3 3 2 6 6 2 2 2 6 6 2 2 2 2 2 2 2 3 3 2 7 7 1 1 2 2 2 2
1 1 2 2 2 2 2 2 2 2 2 2 2 2 2 3 5 2 2 2 2 2 5 3 1 3 5 2
7 2 1 1 1 1 1 1 1 1 2 2 2 2 3 3 2 2 5 3 2 3 3 1 3 3 2
7 2 7 7 7 7 7 7 7 7 1 1 1 1 1 1 2 2 2 3 3 2 2 2 2 1 1 2
```

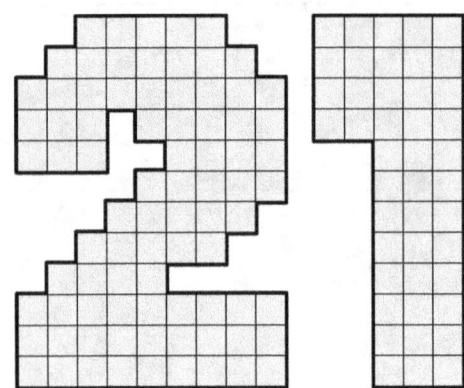

18-1-20-20-12-5-19-14-1-11-5

Suggested Colors

1	red-orange	SO
2	light blue	OVB
3	dark green	KL
4	light gray	CNG
5	black	TB
6	brown	WB

Back-up Colors

1	red
2	blue
3	green
4	gray or orange
5	black
6	brown

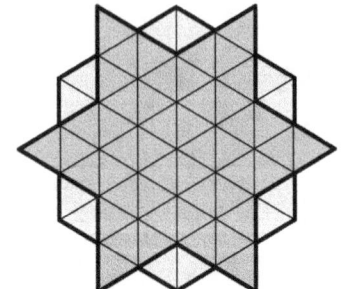 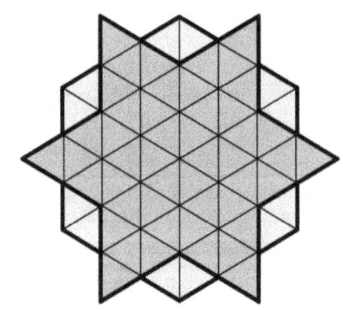 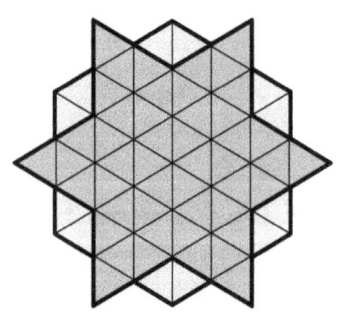

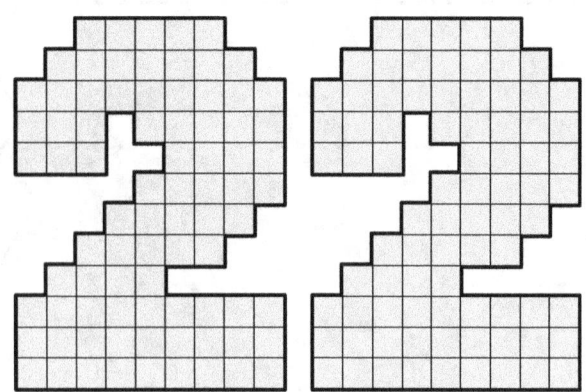

19-5-1-8-15-18-19-5-19

Suggested Colors

1	red	SO
2	dark green	KL
3	black	TB
4	peach	PePa
5	purple	PlPu
6	light blue	MB
7	yellow	YB

Back-up Colors

1	red
2	green
3	black
4	orange
5	purple
6	blue
7	yellow

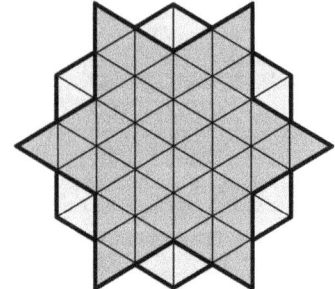
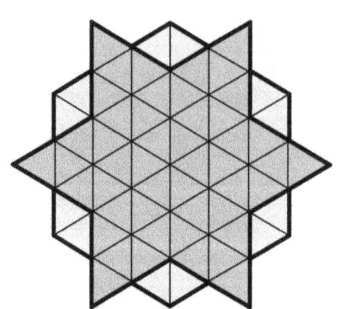
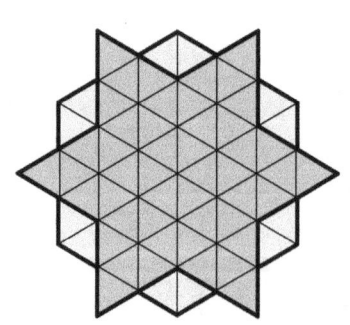

Create Your Own Grid Art!

Now it's your turn to use grids to create amazing art-work! Grids can be used to create eye-popping designs. Try coloring the shapes in different <u>patterns</u> to see what happens.

As you create your artwork, try to fill the whole grid. If you are making an <u>illustration</u> of something or someone, don't forget to add a <u>background</u>.

Pay attention to colors that <u>contrast</u> with each other. Colors that contrast look very different from each other to the human eye. In this book, contrasting colors are used to make the picture stand out from the background. Picture #4 is a good example.

Other Types of Grid Art

Many forms of art use grids. For example, a <u>mosaic</u> (mo-ZAKE) is a piece of art made of many small stones or <u>tiles</u> of different colors, arranged to create patterns and pictures. Mosaics are one of the most ancient forms of artwork.

<u>Embroidery</u> is colored threads sewn onto a piece of cloth to make a design. In some types of embroidery, like cross-stitch and needlepoint, pictures are made from the square grid formed by the woven cloth.

How to Make a Design on a Grid

Here is the secret method that was used to design the scenes in this book. <u>Computer graphics</u> software was used to create the pictures on the previous pages, but you can do the exact same thing with paper.

First, find or draw a color picture to use as a model. It should be about the same size as the grid. As you create this picture, think about the colors you will use in the final grid picture.

Next, lay the picture under the grid. Tape the grid to the picture at the edges so it can't slip.

Finally, fill in each grid shape with the color beneath it. One way to make this easier is to carefully remove the page with the blank grid from the book, then tape the grid and the picture to a sunny window. The bright sunlight will make the picture easier to see.

Many shapes will have more than one color under them. You will have to make a decision about which color looks best with the rest of the picture.

We printed the words on the next few pages a light gray so you can use still this method.

Facts about
Square Grids

A flat surface, like a page in a book, is called a plane. An arrangement of shapes that cover a plane without overlapping is called a tiling. A tiling with a repeating pattern is called a tessellation (tess-uh-LAY-shun). All tessellations are tilings, but not all tilings are tessellations.

Shapes made of straight lines are called polygons, and shapes that are exactly the same shape and size are congruent (con-GREW-ent) to each other. Every grid in this book is a tessellation of congruent polygons, and in every one, the edges all line up and the corners all meet. When the shapes are squares, the grid is sometimes called a quad or quadrille (kwah-DRILL) tiling.

In this book, each square grid is 28 squares wide and 40 squares high and contains a total of 1,120 tiles. That may seem like a lot, but it actually has the fewest tiles of any of the grids in this book!

Squares are regular polygons. A regular polygon is a polygon whose sides are all the same length and whose corners all have the same angle. The quadrille grid is one of only three possible grids that can be made of congruent regular polygons with edges lining up and corners meeting. These three grid patterns are called regular tilings.

Shapes made of square tiles connected at the sides are called polyominoes (polly-OM-in-ohs).

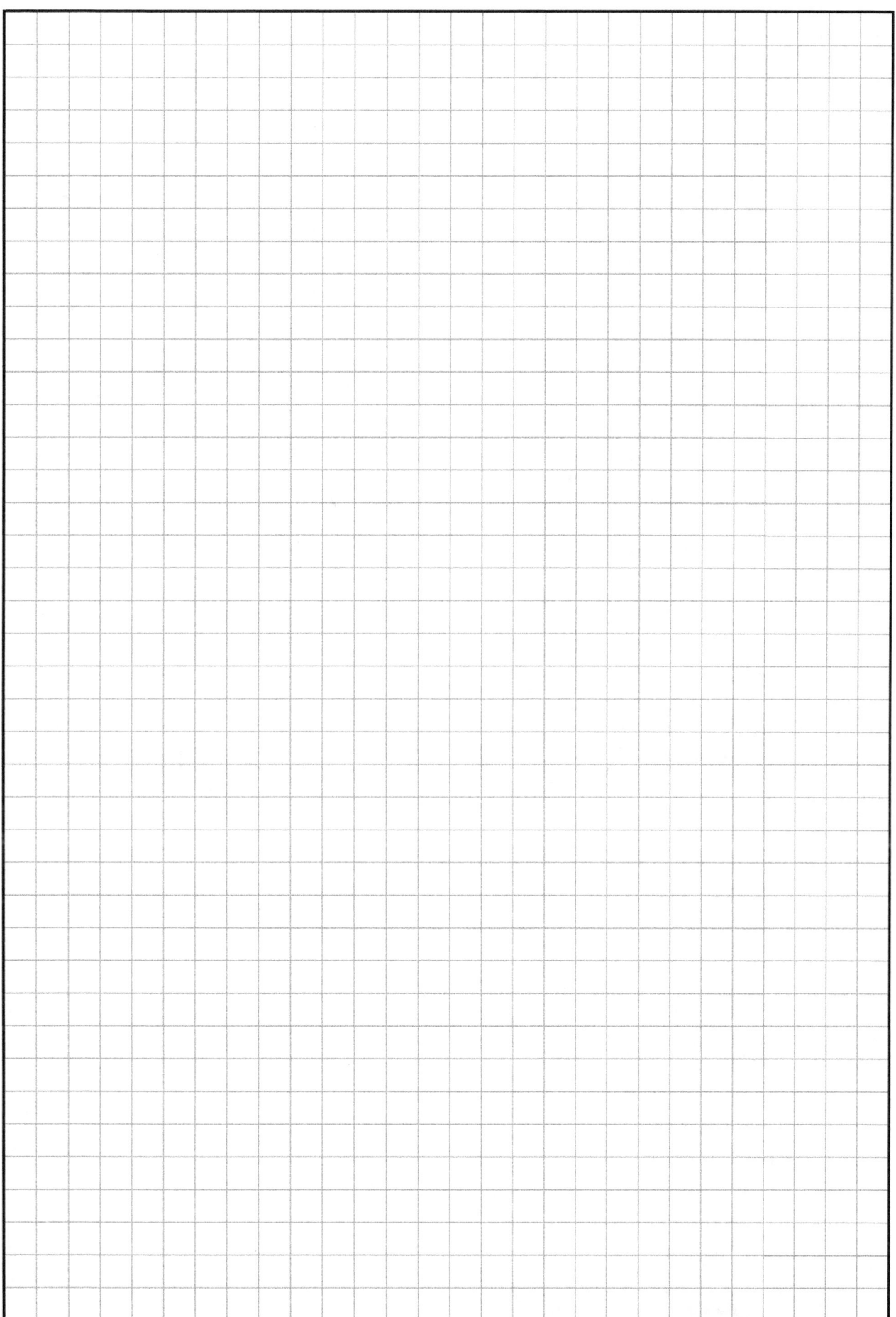

Square Grids in the World

Mosaics often use square grids. So does cross-stitch embroidery. They are also used in computer graphics, where pictures are made of tiny grids of square "dots" called pixels.

Square grids are used for making graphs in mathematics, especially in algebra and calculus. This type of graph uses the Cartesian coordinate system, which was invented by the French mathematician René Descartes. People who need to make graphs sometimes use special graph paper called quad-ruled or quadrille paper, which has a square grid printed on it.

Many pencil puzzles, like crosswords and sudoku, use square grids. Tic-tac-toe is another pencil-and-paper game using this grid shape. Square grids are used in many board games, from chess and checkers to Battleship®. The computer game Tetris® uses polyominoes made of four squares, called tetrominoes.

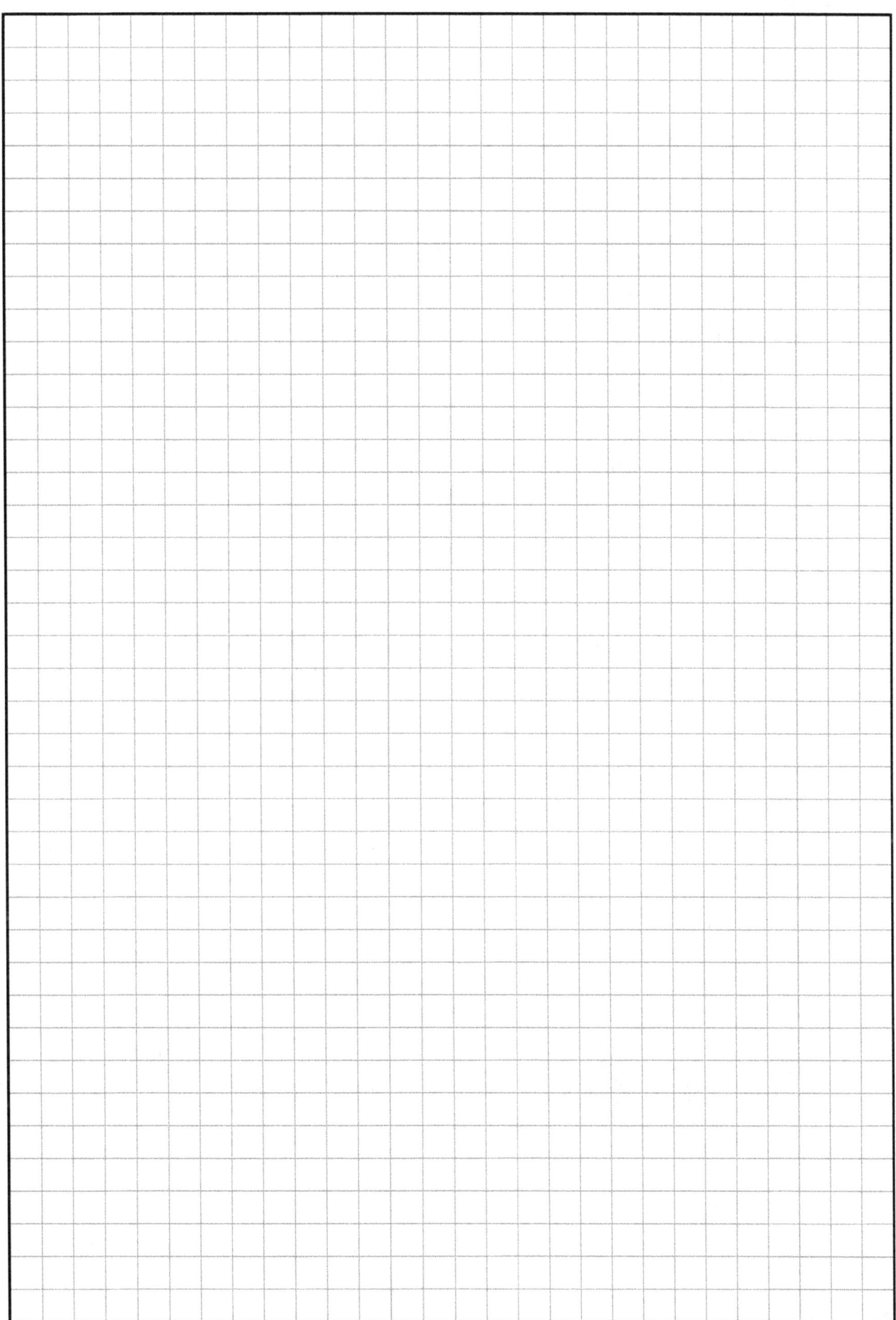

Making Art with a Square Grid

Horizontal (straight across) and vertical (straight up-and-down) lines work very well on the square grid. But diagonal lines on this grid have a jagged, zig-zag edge. Round shapes look blocky.

It's easy to make art on a square grid using a computer. Just use any paint program and zoom in on the picture so that the pixels look like squares.

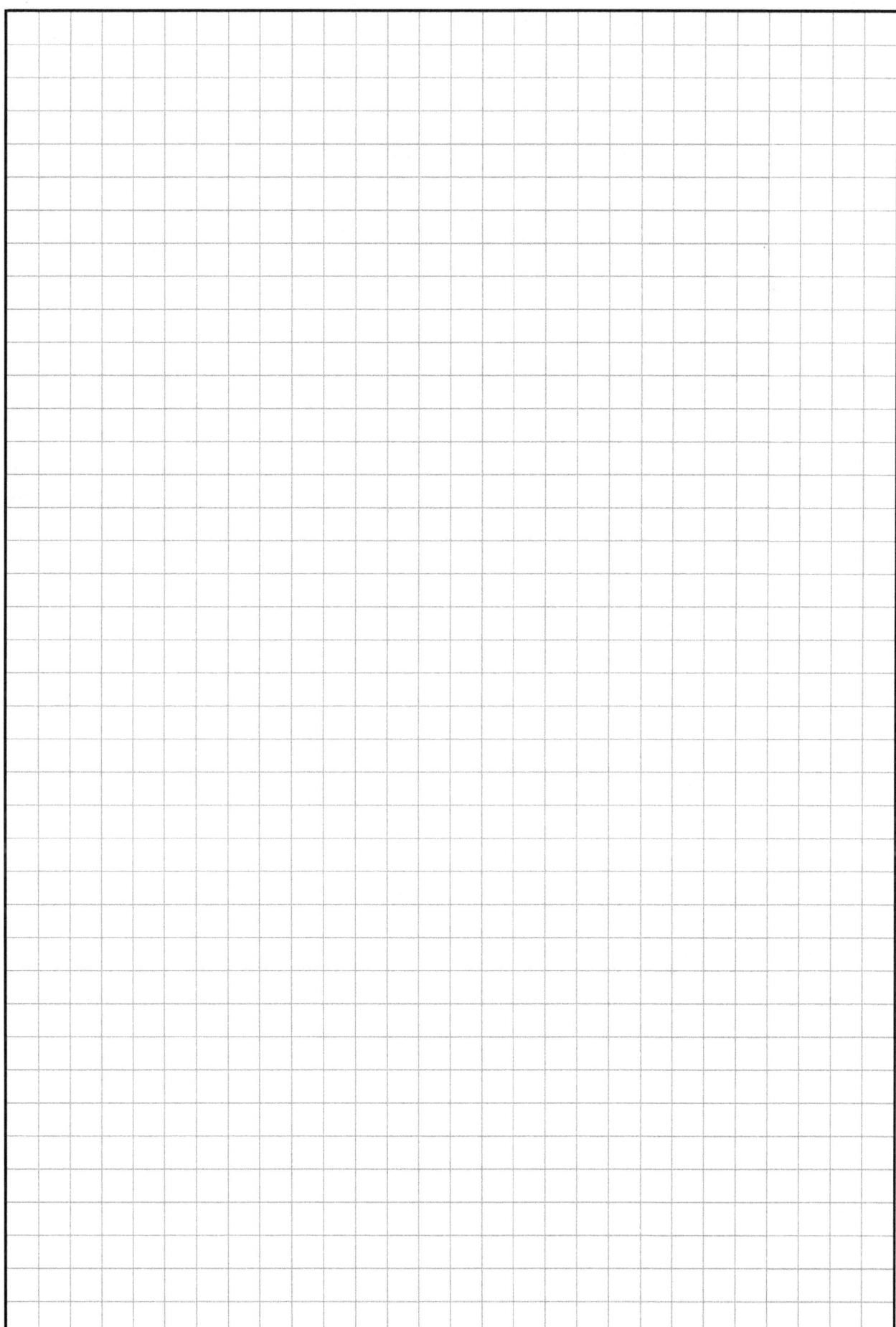

Facts about
Diagonal Square Grids

This grid is made of squares that are criss-crossed with diagonal lines to form triangles. It's 21 squares wide and 30 squares high. With four triangular tiles per square, it contains a total of 2,520 tiles!

Mathematicians call this kind of grid a "tetrakis square tiling" or a "kisquadrille."

This is the only grid in this book made of polygons that have sides of different lengths. All the triangles are congruent, but they face four different ways.

These tiles are isosceles (eye-SOSS-uh-leez) triangles, which means that two of their sides are equal. They are also right triangles, which means that one of their corners is a right angle — in other words, the corner is "square".

Diagonal Square Grids
in the World

Many traditional quilts use a diagonal square grid. Classic <u>quilt blocks</u> using this grid include the hourglass, pinwheel, weather vane, ribbon star, friendship star, flying geese, granny square, and rolling stone.

The playing boards of many games from around the world use a kisquadrille grid. The ancient game alquerque (al-KER-key) was played in Egypt in 600 B.C. and is still played today. Some other kisquadrille games are fanorona (Madagascar), jaguar-and-dogs (South America), zamma (North Africa), sixteen soldiers (Sri Lanka), and tigers-and-goats (Nepal).

Making Art with a Diagonal Square Grid

Of all the grids in this book, the diagonal square grid has the smallest tiles. Its tiles also have the sharpest corners. This makes the diagonal square grids a little harder to color than grids of other shapes. On the other hand, they can also have more detail than any of the other grids.

Any picture made on a regular square grid can also be made on a diagonal square grid. And a pattern from this grid can be turned sideways at a 45° angle, so that one of the corners of the page is pointing straight up. In order to do this, the picture will be made almost 50% larger.

Unlike a regular square tiling, this grid allows smooth diagonal lines of tiles. Zig-zagging lines and <u>chevrons</u> (SHEV-rons), or V-shapes, can be drawn as well.

Try to discover different shapes hidden in the grid. Some possibilities are pinwheels, diamonds, and stars.

Facts about Equilateral Triangle Grids

This grid is made of equilateral (ee-kwah-LAT-er-uhl) triangles. "Equilateral" means that all the sides have the same length. This grid is 39 tiles wide and 33 tiles high, with a total of 1,287 tiles.

Equilateral triangles are always regular polygons, so this is one of the three regular tilings. It also contains another regular tiling hidden inside: the regular hexagon tiling! Six triangles that share a corner make a regular hexagon.

For shapes made from equilateral triangles connected edge-to-edge, the word polyiamond (polly-EYE-mund) was created. Two connected triangle tiles make a diamond, three make a triamond (TRY-mund), and four make a tetriamond (tet-RYE-mund).

Equilateral Triangle Grids in the World

Gardeners often use grids of equilateral triangles to find out how to pack the largest number of plants in their garden without placing any of them too close together.

Triangle grids are used in only a few games. One of them is Chinese checkers, which uses a grid of equilateral triangles arranged to form a large six-pointed star. Blokus® Trigon® is a game that uses polyiamonds on a triangle grid.

Making Art with an Equilateral Triangle Grid

Vertical lines of tiles don't work very well on this grid. Either some tiles will be connected only at the points, making a chain of diamonds, or the line will zig-zag. Only horizontal and diagonal lines of tiles will be straight and smooth. If you turn the page on its side, you can make smooth vertical lines, but not horizontal ones.

Any picture made on a regular hexagon grid can also be made on an equilateral triangle grid, but it will be much larger because each hexagon will contain six triangles.

Many interesting designs can be made on a triangle grid. Try creating polyiamonds like diamonds and stars. Or try making a repeating pattern by using certain colors only on every second, third, or fourth triangle in each row.

Facts About
Regular Hexagon Grids

This grid is made of regular <u>hexagons</u> (polygons with six sides). It is one of the three regular tilings.

In a regular hexagon grid, the tiles are <u>offset</u> from each other. In other words, each row is only halfway down from the row above. Also, the tiles in each row do not touch each other. This the regular hexagon grid different from the other two regular tilings, the square grid and the equilateral triangle grid.

Counting the hexagons in two offset rows, the hexagon grids in this book are 31 tiles wide. Counting the hexagons in the taller columns, they're 38 tiles high. Each grid contains a total of 1,162 tiles.

A shape made of connected hexagons from this grid is called a <u>polyhex</u> (POL-lee-hecks). And all regular hexagons are polyiamonds because they are made of six equilateral triangles. So every polyhex is also a polyiamond!

Regular Hexagon Grids in the World

The regular hexagon tiling is common in nature. For example, bubbles of the same size on the surface of water naturally become arranged into a hexagon grid. And in beehives, the cells of a honeycomb are arranged in a regular hexagon grid. The bees build them this way because this grid shape lets them fit the largest number of cells into a space than any other grid shape. They also need to use the least wax to build the sides of any grid shape.

Graphite (GRAFF-ite) is the black material used in pencil lead. Graphite is made of carbon atoms connected to each other in the shape of hexagon grids, stacked one on top of another. (Coincidentally, the cross-section of many pencils is a regular hexagon!)

The Settlers of Catan®, a popular board game, uses a grid of hexagon-shaped tiles. Many other games, especially computer games and role-playing games, use regular hexagon grids to create maps. In fact, game designers like this grid so much that they have a shortened name for it: hex grid.

Making Art With a
Regular Hexagon Grid

Perfectly smooth lines of tiles are impossible with a hexagon grid. Both straight lines and curves will be bumpy. In the grids in this book, straight bumpy lines can be made vertically and diagonally, but not horizontally. If you turn the grid on its side, bumpy horizontal lines can be made, but not vertical ones.

On the other hand, rounded shapes are easier to make in the hexagon grid than in any other grid shape. Round shapes will be bumpy, but not jagged or spiky. It's also the best grid shape for adding spots, freckles, or polka dots!

Facts About Diamond Grids

A <u>rhombus</u> (ROM-bus) is an equilateral polygon with four sides. This grid is made of a total of 1,514 rhombus tiles. All squares are rhombuses, but some rhombuses (like the ones in this grid) are not squares, because the corners do not all have the same angle. In other words, they are not regular polygons.

In everyday speech, a rhombus that is not a square is sometimes called a <u>lozenge</u> (LOZ-enj) or diamond. The diamonds in this grid are the same shape as polyiamonds made from two equilateral triangles. The diamond grid pattern used in this book is called a rhombille (rom-BILL) tiling.

Like the equilateral triangle grid, this grid contains a hidden hexagon grid. Each hexagon is made from three diamonds.

The diamonds of a rhombille grid can be colored to look like cubes. In the grids in this book, this <u>illusion</u> is easiest to see if you turn the page on its side.

Diamond Grids
in the World

In quilting, a rhombille tiling pattern colored to look like cubes is called a <u>tumbling block</u> pattern. The ancient Greeks sometimes used tumbling blocks in floor mosaics using three different colors of diamond-shaped tiles. Some of these interesting mosaics still exist today.

The floor of the cathedral in Siena, Italy is famous for its mosaics, which include a rhombille tiling. Unlike the more ancient Greek mosaics, the diamond-shaped tiles in the rhombille part of the cathedral floor are all identical.

The classic video game Q*bert™ used a rhombille grid colored to look like a <u>pyramid</u> of cubes. Only the tops of the cubes were used in the game play, but the game designers wanted the game's graphics to have an illusion of being in 3D.

The rhombille tiling can be found in all three pieces in series <u>Metamorphosis</u> by the artist M. C. Escher. Escher is famous for using tessellations in much of his artwork.

Making Art With a Diamond Grid

This may be the trickiest grid for creating illustrations. Good pictures for this grid include things with spiky or pointy shapes. Try fish (with the scales), insects, flowers, airplanes, or spaceships.

Some unusual patterns can be created on the diamond grid. Test out different ways of coloring the diamonds to create six-pointed stars, zig-zags, strings of beads, and more.

Geometry
Vocabulary Words

angle

Cartesian coordinate system

congruent

equilateral

graph

hexagon

isosceles

plane

polygon

polyhex

polyiamond

polyomino

quadrille

pyramid

regular polygon

regular tiling

rhombus

right angle

right triangle

tessellation

tiling

Art & Design
Vocabulary Words

background

chevron

computer graphics

contrast

cross-section

embroidery

graphite

horizontal

illusion

illustration

lozenge

mosaic

offset

pattern

pixel

quilt block

tile

tumbling block

vertical

zoom

www.ingramcontent.com/pod-product-compliance
Lightning Source LLC
Chambersburg PA
CBHW080947170526

45158CB00008B/2398